Communication Through Writing

Margaret Pogemiller Coffey

University of Kansas Applied English Center

Photographs by Haissam M. Chehab

PRENTICE HALL REGENTS, Englewood Cliffs, NJ 07632

Library of Congress Cataloging-in-Publication Data

COFFEY, MARGARET POGEMILLER.
  Communication through writing.

  Includes index.
    1. English language—Rhetoric. 2. English
language—Textbooks for foreign speakers. I. Title.
PE1408.C54324 1987   808'.042   86-30624
ISBN 0-13-152984-6

Communication Through Writing is for the ESL faculty at Donnelly College. Their dedication to their profession, their program, and their students will be a never-ending source of inspiration to me.

Editorial/production supervision and
   interior design: Patricia V. Amoroso
Cover design: Bruce Kenselaar
Cover photograph: Haissam M. Chehab
Manufacturing buyer: Margaret Rizzi

Printed in the United States of America

10 9 8 7 6 5 4 3

ISBN 0-13-152984-6   01

PRENTICE-HALL INTERNATIONAL (UK) LIMITED, *London*
PRENTICE-HALL OF AUSTRALIA PTY. LIMITED, *Sydney*
PRENTICE-HALL CANADA INC., *Toronto*
PRENTICE-HALL HISPANOAMERICANA, S.A., *Mexico City*
PRENTICE-HALL OF INDIA PRIVATE LIMITED, *New Delhi*
PRENTICE-HALL OF JAPAN, INC., *Tokyo*
PRENTICE-HALL OF SOUTHEAST ASIA PTE. LTD., *Singapore*
EDITORA PRENTICE-HALL DO BRASIL, LTDA., *Rio de Janeiro*

Contents

To the Instructor

Communication Through Writing is a writing text for English-language learners. It is intended for high-intermediate and low-advanced students in preacademic programs and for advanced students in adult programs. In a series of twelve chapters, *Communication Through Writing* reviews the paragraph and then introduces the short essay and basic writing patterns used in the short essay (such as illustration, comparison and contrast, and persuasion). The instructor's manual that accompanies the text gives more detailed suggestions on how to use the material in each chapter.

The objective of the text is to make clear that writing—in this case the short essay—is an effective means of communication. It has been the author's experience in the classroom that students learning English find writing either "scary" or "just something to put up with" until the end of their language training. This text hopes to change these notions by showing that writing is a form of communication in which one meaningfully expresses, for example, ideas, hopes, opinions, and findings to other people. In addition, the text attempts to teach students that writing is the end result of a *process* in which one thinks, discusses with others, writes, gets feedback on the writing, and then rewrites one or several times. It is hoped that through lots of actual writing experience students will begin to see that the writing process is fun rather than painful and results in meaningful communication.

SIGNIFICANT FEATURES OF THE TEXT

The sections that follow provide an overview of the significant features presented in *Communication Through Writing.*

Writing as a Process

Communication Through Writing gives a clear presentation of the steps in the writing process so that students can identify and begin to use them. Too often English-as-a-second-language (ESL) writers at this level feel a great sense of frustration when asked to compose a piece of writing because they know quite a bit of grammar and vocabulary and are able to formulate complex thoughts in English yet have a difficult time translating this information onto the written page. This may be because they have not learned three important steps in the writing process: the careful and deliberate *formulation* and *organization* of the information before writing and the *editing* of information once it has been written. *Communication Through Writing* provides students with the opportunity to complete these three often missing steps. In each writing activity, they think about the writing assignment, work with peers to gain important information and feedback on ideas, and outline the acquired material before they ever start writing. Once the first draft is composed, students follow a specific step in which they check their material with an outside source in a section called "Peer Editing." Here, students are expected to re-evaluate formally what they have written before producing a final draft. By presenting all the steps in a writing activity, the text gives students a realistic idea of how to compose an essay.

The Interactive Nature of Writing

This text also emphasizes that writing is interactive in nature; one's peers can be a good source of information and feedback. Students too often have the idea that writing is a kind of "two-dimensional" activity that occurs only between the student and the instructor: The student writes and the teacher evaluates what is written. *Communication Through Writing* provides a better approach by showing that the best writing comes after one has had a chance to think about and discuss pertinent ideas with other people. These other people can be anyone able to provide helpful information: a classmate, a librarian, an instructor, even a next-door neighbor. This interaction is one means of exciting a student about essay writing. The student begins to realize that the reason one writes is because one has something valuable to express, and one has something valuable to express because one first formulated worthwhile ideas while thinking and working with others.

Writing Strategies

A third significant feature of *Communication Through Writing* is its presentation of basic writing strategies commonly used to gather information and ideas for a writing assignment. Preceding the text, in the section entitled "Strategies for Gathering Information," is a glossary of the strategies that will be used: *brainstorming, interviewing, listmaking, observing, roleplaying on paper,* and *WH-questioning.* The glossary defines each strategy and then explains why and how the writer uses it. In the guided writing activity in each chapter, students are asked to use one or more of these writing strategies to gather ideas for their paper. This is a very important feature of the book because it teaches students how to get over the hurdle of "writer's block" when they simply cannot come up with any ideas. Learning the writing strategies helps eliminate much of the fear or mystery in writing. It shows students that there are systematic devices that writers use to generate information.

Final Instructor-Writer Discussions

A fourth distinctive feature of this text appears at the end of each guided writing activity. Here, students are deliberately asked to discuss their composition with their instructor once it has been evaluated. The author realizes that this may not be easy to accomplish, particularly in large classes. However, it will probably not be as difficult as one might first imagine because in the writing process students will be relying more on each other than on their teacher. Also, students will most likely not be finishing writing assignments at the same time. This should free the instructor to meet with students on an individual basis, even during class time. If at all possible, finding time for this step is strongly encouraged because it provides an opportunity for student and teacher to communicate directly and regularly about the student's writing strengths and weaknesses. It is a means by which teachers can be sure that students are really examining the written evaluation. It reinforces the instructor's care of the student's writing. In addition, it provides further emphasis that writing is an interactive process from beginning to end.

Supplemental Writing Assignments

The last significant feature of this text is its final chapter. In it students are given first thesis statements, then essay topics, and finally categories of subjects that can be developed into short essays. There is no guidance as to how this is to be done. It is the student's responsibility to apply what he or she has learned in the first eleven chapters in order to write valuable, interesting essays. This last chapter is a strong feature of a composition textbook because it gives students a realistic picture of how they will be expected to use their composition skills in the future. Outside of composition class, students will probably not be told that the best way to express a particular idea is to classify it, to compare and contrast it with another idea, or to use a combination of the two. The student will have to take the writing patterns and strategies he or she knows and learn to present the information in the most logical and comprehensible manner possible. This chapter is distinctive because very few texts include one like it. This chapter is important because it brings the instructions of the process of essay writing to a close: In the beginning of the book, students are presented with the structure of the essay, then they are guided step-by-step through the patterns and process used in essay writing, and finally they are given a chance to produce essays on their own, which is the goal of teaching compositions skills in the first place.

WORKING THROUGH A CHAPTER

With the exception of the first chapter (which introduces the paragraph and the short essay) and the last chapter (which gives a variety of supplemental unguided writing assignments), the approach to teaching essay writing skills is the same in each chapter. It is as follows:

1. *An introduction to the writing pattern.* As briefly as possible, the text explains what the writing pattern is and why it is used. This gives students a chance to focus on and discuss the type of writing that will be covered in the chapter. The amount of time spent presenting the writing pattern will, of course, depend on the needs of the students. It is suggested, however, that teachers move through this section as quickly as possible. It is meant to be a reference point for the students as they practice the writing pattern throughout the remainder of the chapter.

2. *Exercises on the writing pattern.* These exercises give students practical experience with the writing pattern before they are expected to use it in their writing activity at the end of the chapter.

3. *Important vocabulary.* In this section students are presented helpful words and phrases for the particular writing pattern they are learning. Several sample sentences are included. The text attempts to present the vocabulary items as logically as possible (grouping verb phrases as a unit, grouping noun phrases as a unit, separating words of comparison from words of contrast, and so on) to help students more quickly understand how they function in a sentence.

4. *Vocabulary exercises.* These give students directed practice using the vocabulary they have just learned before they are expected to use it in their writing activity at the end of the chapter.

5. *Important punctuation/usage.* In this section the students' attention is focused on punctuation and usage rules that help one achieve accuracy in sentence structure. This section places emphasis on sentence-level problems: explaining correct formation of the compound, complex, and simple sentences; correct use of the comma, colon, and semicolon; differences between main clauses and subordinate clauses; and so on.

6. *Punctuation/usage exercises.* These exercises give students directed practice using the punctuation and usage rules at the sentence level before they are expected to use them in their writing activity at the end of the chapter.

7. *Writing practice.* In each chapter students are given a step-by-step guided writing activity. This series of steps is used because it has been found to lead to a successful end: well-written short essays. Of course, instructors should feel free to modify the suggested process to best help their students. The process is as follows:

    a. Introduction to the writing activity
    b. Peer interaction work/Writing strategies work
    c. Organization of the information the writer has acquired
    d. Rough draft
    e. Peer-editing activity
    f. Composition of the final draft
    g. Discussion of work with the instructor.

8. *Additional topics.* At the end of each chapter, students are given approximately seven additional topics providing practice on the writing pattern they have just learned. These topics are not guided. However, it is intended that the instructor will encourage students during their composition writing to use what they have learned regarding the writing pattern, language structure, and vocabulary and will encourage them to work consciously through the steps of the writing process.

Strategies for Gathering Information

We write because we have something to express. However, it is not realistic to expect that the ideas will always flow logically and easily from our minds just because we want to write. In fact, the opposite is more common. How many times have you sat with a pen in your hand staring at a blank piece of paper, not able to think of a single sentence to put on the paper?

In this text you will learn that writers use strategies (aids) to help them gather information and ideas that can then be logically put into a paper. Using these writing strategies is an important step in the writing process. Following are the six we will use in *Communication Through Writing*. Discuss each one with your instructor. Ask questions if you do not understand.

BRAINSTORMING

When brainstorming, you try to think of anything that comes to mind on a certain topic. There are no "good" or "bad" ideas in brainstorming. Any idea you have is acceptable. You don't have to think carefully or write grammatically perfect sentences. You don't have to put your thoughts in a specific order. The point is to come up with as much information as possible. This information can include diagrams, pictures, single words, phrases, and sentences. Don't worry about what the page of notes looks like. When you are finished, you can organize your brainstorming information into a useful order.

INTERVIEWING

When interviewing, you gather information from a person who is knowledgeable on your essay topic. The benefit of interviewing is that it allows you to gather information for your paper that you might not know from your own experience. Here are some points to consider before interviewing:

a. At the beginning of the interview, introduce yourself and explain what you are doing.

b. Know in advance the basic questions you want to ask, but be prepared to add new questions in the interview.

c. Take good notes or record the interview. It is dangerous to assume that you will remember the conversation after the interview.

d. Don't worry about writing perfect English sentences. Don't try to decide which information is useful. Once the interview is over, you can decide which ideas you want to use.

LISTMAKING

Listmaking is similar to brainstorming in that you gather a lot of information in a short amount of time. Listmaking is different, however, in that you try to identify the different steps, parts, or examples of one category. You might, for example, be asked to write down all the problems at your school. You don't give a lot of detail in listmaking. That is what you do in brainstorming. Often a writer will make a list of items on a topic and then brainstorm about each one individually.

When listmaking, you don't have to arrange your information in any certain order or use perfect English. You don't have to evaluate the items on your list as being useful or useless. After you have finished listmaking, you can decide which information to keep or throw away and in which order to put it.

OBSERVING

In this writing strategy you observe a person, place, or object and then write down what you hear, smell, see, and so on. This writing strategy is particularly helpful when describing something in an essay. It helps you get the information you might not think of on your own. When observing, take a lot of paper and a pencil to the location. For a few minutes sit and notice what is around you. When you feel familiar with your surroundings, start taking notes. You don't have to think carefully or write grammatically perfect sentences. You don't have to put your thoughts in a specific order. Just gather as much information as possible. When you are finished observing and are ready to start organizing your essay, then you can decide which information to keep.

ROLEPLAYING ON PAPER

This writing strategy could also be called "a conversation on paper." When using it, you are two people: yourself and another person who has valuable ideas to add to your topic. To create ideas, you and the other person actually "talk" to each other on paper. If you wanted to write about a problem at your school, for example, you might have a conversation between yourself and your advisor. First you would discuss the problem as yourself. Then you would discuss the problem as your advisor. In the first part you would actually think and react as yourself; in the other part of the conversation you would think and react as the other person.

Writers use this strategy to help them see a topic in ways they might normally not. It particularly helps writers gather information about a point of view with which they disagree.

When roleplaying on paper just write any information that comes to your mind during the "conversation." You don't have to evaluate your ideas as being useful or useless. After you have finished roleplaying, you can decide which ideas you want to keep or throw away.

WH-QUESTIONS

The WH-Question strategy is a specific kind of listmaking. It is particularly helpful when you are writing a story. On a piece of paper you make columns for each WH-Question.

WHO	*WHAT*	*WHERE*	*WHEN*	*WHY*	*HOW*

Then you gather all the information you can think of about your story for each question. In other words you give information for *who* is in the story, *what* the story is about, *where* the story happens, and so on. The point is to gather as much information as possible about your story. You don't have to arrange the information for each question in any certain order. You don't have to use perfect English or worry about whether the information is useful or useless. Just put down any ideas you think will help make your story complete and interesting. After you have finished, you can decide which information you want to keep or throw away.

Transitions: Words That Link One Idea to Another

Following are transitions that help writers put ideas in a logical order. This reference list of common transitions is for you to use while writing. For a more complete explanation of how to use these transitions and other vocabulary expressions, read the Important Vocabulary section in each chapter.

Transitions to Show Time (see page 23)

Beginning of a Time Sequence

In the beginning,

At first,

At the start,

First of all,

Middle of a Time Sequence

Next,

After that,

Then,

Second, Third, etc.

Following,

Subsequently,

End of a Time Sequence

Eventually,

At last,

In conclusion,

Finally,

To sum up,

As has been noted,

Relationship of One Time to Another (see pages 23–24 and 73)

During

When

While

As soon as

As

The minute that

At the same time

Before

Until

After

As

Afterwards

Following that

Transitions to Show Location (spatial order) (see pages 39–40)

on, at, in

under, beneath

over, on top of, at the top of, on the side of, at the bottom of

inside, outside

beside, next to, near, in between

in back of, in the middle of, in front of

(to) (on) the left (of), (to) (on) the right (of)

across from

(at) (on) the corner of

at the end of

Transitions to Illustrate a General Idea (see page 58)

Generally (speaking),

In general

On the whole,

For the most part,

As a rule

It is widely accepted that

Transitions to Illustrate a Specific Idea (see pages 58–59)

For example,
As an (another) example,
As an (another) illustration,
Specifically,
In particular,
Namely,
That is,
To illustrate,

Transitions to Emphasize an Idea (to show one idea as being more important than others) (see pages 59–60)

Above all,
Especially,
Most important,

Transitions to Compare Ideas (see page 113)

Similarly,
In the same way,
Likewise,
Correspondingly,

Transitions to Contrast Ideas (see page 114)

However,
On the other hand,
On the contrary,
In contrast,
While
Whereas
Although

Transitions to Show a Result (see page 97)

So, Thus
Therefore,
Consequently,
As a consequence,
For this reason,
As a result,

1

Introduction to the Short Essay

Writing, like speaking, is an important means of communication. In fact, sometimes the written word is the only acceptable way to communicate. A corporation might, for example, require a written letter of introduction before granting you a job interview. You might need to make a formal complaint to a company or a person. Many places will not consider a complaint or request unless it is made in written form. Your philosophy instructor could ask you to write an essay exam, or you may have to do a written research report in your major field of study. In the North American culture, a great deal of emphasis is placed on being able to express one's ideas well in written form.

When it comes to making yourself understood, speaking has some advantages that writing does not. As an example, when you speak to a person, you can use nonverbal body language to help make your point. You can also ask for immediate feedback from your listener to make sure he or she understands. You can even keep repeating and revising what you are saying until you can send precisely the message you intended. These aids are not possible when communicating in written form. Once you have given others your written work, you need to feel certain they will understand the point you are trying to make with no further assistance from you. For this reason, there have been established certain standard ways of presenting information in written form that people generally understand. In this text, you are going to learn one of these forms: the *short essay*.

The short essay, or the composition, as it is sometimes called, is a type of writing that concisely makes a point to the reader in approximately 500 words or one and one-half to two written pages. The essay is composed of different parts, thus the name "composition." These parts are called paragraphs and are put together in different manners depending upon how the writer wants to present his or her ideas.

There are several different methods one can use in a short essay to present ideas. These are *basic writing patterns*. You might, for example, want to convince people that smoking is harmful to one's health. In this case, you would use the writing pattern known as persuasion. By the time you finish this book, you will have been introduced to and will have practiced the basic writing patterns in the short essay.

Now let's look at what makes up the short essay.

THE PARAGRAPH

We first need to look at the unit of writing known as the *paragraph*. The paragraph is a group of sentences that clearly and concisely expresses one basic idea. The paragraph can be complete in itself, or it can be a part of an essay, a research report, a book, and so on.

A paragraph looks something like this:

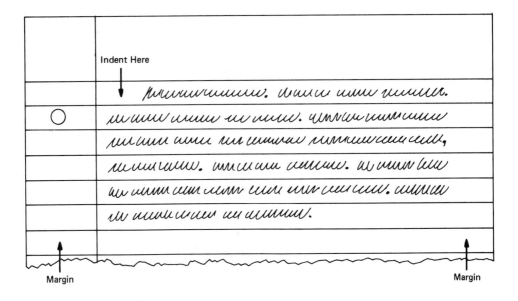

Remember to indent (leave a space) at the beginning of every paragraph. Also remember to leave a margin (a column of space) on both the left- and right-hand sides of the page.

The Basic Parts of the Paragraph

The paragraph has three basic parts: the topic sentence, the developing sentences, and the conclusion. Each part plays a role in writing a good paragraph.

The Topic Sentence

The main idea of the paragraph is stated in the *topic sentence*. It is usually the most general statement of the paragraph but must be specific enough so that it can be adequately covered in the paragraph itself. The topic sentence needs to make a point. It should give an idea that is worth developing further. Although the topic sentence can be located in the middle or the end of the paragraph, it is most commonly found at the beginning. As a new writer of English, you will probably find it easier to put your topic sentence at the beginning of the paragraph.

The Developing Sentences/Unity

The task of the *developing sentences* is to cover completely the idea presented in the topic sentence. No one can say exactly how many sentences that will take. If the idea in your topic is simple, it will take only a few sentences. If your topic sentence presents a more complex idea, it may take many sentences to cover the topic adequately. When a paragraph presents all the information necessary to express an idea and does not make any unnecessary points, we say that is has *unity*.

The Conclusion

The *conclusion* of the paragraph is generally one sentence that brings the development of your idea to a close. It lets the reader know that you have finished discussing this idea.

Coherence

When writing a paragraph, there is one more point to consider: *coherence*. A paragraph has coherence when it is understandable, or makes sense, to the reader. For a paragraph to have coherence, it must present all of its ideas in a logical order. In other words, each sentence needs to flow directly into the one following it. Three very common techniques used by writers to achieve coherence are

1. repetition of key words of phrases

2. transitions

3. pronoun reference.

The *repetition of key words or phrases* means that the writer repeats throughout the paragraph words or phrases that are very important to the main idea. For example, in the following sample paragraph describing the common cold, the writer repeats the words *cold, aches,* and *pain* several times because she is trying to make the point that aches and pains are a major part of any cold (see page 5).

Transitions are special vocabulary words that say to the reader, "We're going from one idea to another." For example, the words *first, next, then, after that,* and *last* are common transitional words used by writers when they want to go from one moment of time to the next in their explanation.

To use *pronoun reference* means to mention a word or phrase and then to refer to it again in pronoun form. For example: *The students* left the classroom at 7:00 P.M. *They* (the students) decided to leave because *their* professor (the students' professor) did not come to class.

One of these techniques or a combination of them can be used in a paragraph to achieve coherence. You will learn more about coherence in the following chapters of the book as you practice the special techniques presented here.

Let's look at the following example of a paragraph.

The First Twenty-Four Hours

I hate the first twenty-four hours of a bad cold. Anyone who has said, "Oh, you just have a little cold" must never have suffered from its aches and pains. To sum it up, when I have a bad cold, I hurt. Even though I am buried under four or five heavy blankets, my feet feel like ice. Rippling[1] up and down my legs, stomach, and arms are hundreds of little goose bumps[2]. They cause me to shake and feel chilly[3] even though inside I feel as if I am burning up. Every muscle in my body, from my feet to my head, aches. It is that terrible dull pain that is constantly there even if I don't move a finger. If I try to ignore my body aches, I am then reminded of my cold by the jabbing[4] pain I feel in my throat when I swallow. The most aggravating[5] part of the cold, however, occurs from my neck up. My head not only hurts, it is messy. I am always sneezing, coughing, blowing my nose, and wiping my watery eyes. It seems as if the plan is to keep a person so busy blowing and wiping that he or she will forget being sick. It doesn't work. So there I lie feeling too sick to move. My doctor doesn't want to see me because what I have "isn't serious." My coworkers and friends don't want to see me because I "might be catching."[6] Who can blame them? I'd give anything not to be around myself during those first twenty-four hours!

Vocabulary

[1]**rippling:** moving in small waves

[2]**goose bumps:** tiny bumps that appear on the skin when one is cold or afraid

[3]**chilly:** to be cold

[4]**jabbing:** very sharp

[5]**aggravating:** unpleasant

[6]**"might be catching":** Someone might get sick from my cold.

Discussion Questions

1. What is the topic of this paragraph? What point is the writer trying to make?

2. Do the developing sentences cover the topic? Explain.

3. Do the developing sentences stay on the topic? In other words, is there any unnecessary information in the paragraph?

4. Considering the answers for 2 and 3, can we say that this paragraph has unity? Explain.

5. Does this paragraph have coherence? In other words, does the writer describe the cold in a logical order that is easy to follow? Explain.

6. Does this paragraph have a good concluding sentence?

7. Do you agree with the writer's description of a cold? What would you add to or change about the description?

EXERCISE 1: Distinguishing Between Strong and Weak Topic Sentences

---

Remember it was stated earlier that a topic sentence is the most general sentence of a paragraph but that it needs to be specific enough to be covered in one paragraph. Look at the following statements. Explain which are good topic sentences and which are not.

EXAMPLE: All maple trees lose their leaves.

This is a weak topic sentence because it is too general and does not really make a point that can be developed into a paragraph. It might be better to say, "Botanists can give a step-by-step explanation why maple trees drop their leaves in the fall."

EXAMPLE: In his song "A Junkie's Lament" James Taylor gives his impressions of the horror of having a heroin addiction.

This is a good topic sentence because it is limited to one idea and the reader knows how the writer plans to develop that idea. The topic sentence states that the paragraph is going to discuss one specific song. The discussion is going to center around the song's negative references to a heroin addiction.

1. One way to learn how to relax is to practice biofeedback at home on a daily basis.

2. Writing a good paragraph is easy.

3. The three best television programs this year were unusual.

4. Riding a motorcycle is different from riding a bicycle in two crucial ways.

5. Women's liberation is evident in every aspect of U.S. society.

6. The Koran is an example of inspired writing.

7. Brown's is the best barbecue restaurant I've ever eaten in because of its service, excellent food, and reasonable prices.

8. Recent scientific research demonstrates that house plants respond positively to classical music but react negatively to rock and roll.

EXERCISE 2: Writing Topic Sentences

The following topic sentences are weak because they are too general to be adequately covered in one paragraph. Try to rewrite the statements so that they make an interesting point about a topic that can be covered in one paragraph.

EXAMPLE: Baseball players make too much money.

When it is reported that a baseball player will earn nine million dollars over the next four years, I believe we have passed what is an acceptable salary for a person in professional sports.

1. Anyone can learn a second language.

   _____

   _____

   _____

2. Drinking too much coffee is bad for you.

   _____

   _____

   _____

3. Los Angeles is an exciting place.

   _____

   _____

   _____

4. Engineering is an excellent major to take in the university.

   _____

   _____

   _____

5. All children can be noisy.

_____

_____

_____

EXERCISE 3: Writing a Paragraph

Following are four topic sentence choices. Choose one and develop a paragraph from it. Remember that after you state your topic sentence, you need to have developing sentences that adequately cover your topic. You also need to have a conclusion. Finally, check to be sure that your paragraph has unity and coherence. When you finish your paragraph, share it with your instructor.

Topic Sentence Selections

1. I can think of two reasons why no person should ever be without a savings account.

2. My favorite sport to participate in is _____ because it gives me the chance to _____.

3. My family is different from other families I know in one way.

4. Your own topic sentence

_____

_____

_____

_____

_____

THE SHORT ESSAY

While the paragraph is a unit of writing composed of several sentences, the short essay is a unit of writing composed of several paragraphs. The short essay usually contains four to eight paragraphs. These paragraphs combine together to express one central idea. An essay is generally a complete work within itself and looks something like this:

Margin   Margin

Title ⟶ *wwwwww wwww*

Indent ⟶ *wwwwwwwwwwwwwwwwwwwww. wwwwwwwwww*

◯ *wwwwwwwwww wwwww www www. wwwwwwwwwww*

wwwwwww wwwww wwwwwww. www wwwwwww wwwwww,

wwwww www wwwwwwwwwwwwww. wwwwwwwwww

wwwwww. wwwwww wwww wwwwwwwww.

Indent ⟶ *wwwwwwww www. wwwwwwwwwwww, wwwwww*

wwwwww wwwwwww wwwwww. www wwwww wwwww.

wwwww www www ww wwwwwww. wwwww

www wwwww wwww wwwww wwwwwww. wwwww

◯ *ww wwwww. wwwwww ww, wwwwww wwww*

wwww www wwww www ww wwww wwwww.

www wwww www wwww.

Indent ⟶ *ww wwwwww ww www wwww. wwww*

ww www ww www www. ww www wwwwwww

www www www wwwwww. www wwwww

www www wwww. www wwwwww. www www

◯ *www wwwwww.*

Remember to indent (leave a space) at the beginning of each paragraph. When you write the last sentence of a paragraph, put a period and do not write any more on that line of paper. Go to the next line, indent, and begin your next paragraph. Also remember to leave a margin (column of space) on both the left- and right-hand sides of the page.

The Basic Parts of the Short Essay

The short essay has five basic parts: the title, the introductory paragraph, the thesis statement, the developing paragraphs, and the concluding paragraph.

The Title

The *title* of the essay is a short phrase that briefly indicates to the reader what the subject of the composition will be. If well-written, it should not simply state the subject but should also make the reader *want* to read the composition. Consider, for example, the following two titles on the same subject:

"Neighborhoods Near Chemical Factories"

"Life-threatening Chemical Risks May Be in Your Own Backyard"

Which essay would you rather read? Why?

The title is written at the top center of the first page of the essay. Generally, in a title all words except articles (*a, an, the*), conjunctions, and prepositions of less than five letters are capitalized. This is not a definite rule, however. If you have any questions, ask your instructor or consult an English grammar handbook.

The Introductory Paragraph and the Thesis Statement

The first paragraph of an essay is the *introductory paragraph*. It is in this paragraph that the writer focuses the reader's attention on the subject of the essay—what will be discussed and how it will be developed. The introductory paragraph contains the *thesis statement*. The thesis statement presents the single basic idea of the composition and explains the author's *purpose* for discussing the subject. In other words, the thesis statement also clearly explains through a personal opinion or a unique point of view why the author thinks this subject is important enough to write about. The thesis statement generally presents a point that can adequately be developed in approximately four to eight paragraphs. The last function of the thesis statement is to introduce very briefly the points that will be covered in the essay. As you can see, the thesis statement is very important because it controls how the rest of the composition will be developed.

The Developing Paragraphs

The *developing paragraphs*, which follow the introduction, are sometimes called the *body* of the essay. These are the paragraphs where the writer adequately supports the point made in the thesis statement. To do this the writer can use many types of information, including examples, facts, statistics, opinions, and descriptive and narrative details. These developing paragraphs use different types of writing patterns to present the information. In one essay, for example, your developing paragraphs might classify the different parts of your central idea. In another essay, these paragraphs might discuss the causes and effects of something happening. The type of writing pattern you decide to use depends on how you want to develop the idea in your thesis statement. We will learn more about the different writing patterns later in the text.

Remember that each paragraph should have a topic sentence that is supported by well-developed ideas. Review in this chapter the section on the paragraph if you have forgotten.

The Concluding Paragraph

The last part of the essay is the *concluding paragraph*. It is generally short and simply stated. The aim of this paragraph is to let your reader know that you are bringing your ideas to a close. It also gives you a chance to restate the main idea presented in the thesis statement. Sometimes in the conclusion a writer will give special emphasis to the purpose of the essay (often in the form of a quotation or a personal opinion). When effectively done, this can create an impressive conclusion to the development of your thesis statement.

Remember earlier we learned that when writing a paragraph, it is important to be concerned with coherence and unity. This is also the case when writing an essay. For an essay to have unity, each paragraph in it must help develop the thesis statement completely. When the reader finishes the essay, he or she should not feel that any important information is missing. In addition, for an essay to have unity, the paragraphs cannot present any information that does not in some way support the thesis statement. Simply stated, having unity means staying on the subject and developing it fully.

An essay has coherence when all its paragraphs are presented in a logical order. The introduction, each developing paragraph, and the conclusion must present the content of the essay in a way that the reader can easily follow. This could mean, for example, presenting information in a logical sequence of time, in a logical sequence of space, or in a logical sequence of general to specific ideas. If the information in the essay is not presented in a reasonable and ordered way, the point the writer is trying to make will not be clear and may even be lost. Like paragraphs, essays often use transition words, pronoun reference, and repetition of important words to help the ideas flow from one sentence to the next and from one paragraph to the next. We will learn more about these techniques in the chapters that follow.

Now look at the sample essay here.

The Forgotten Letter

We Americans have forgotten how to write letters as a means of keeping in touch over long distances with people we care about. This is sad but not at all surprising. The principle cause for our shift away from letter writing can be summed up[1] in two words: the telephone. The telephone has caused us to put away our pens and paper because it is generally more convenient and immediately gratifying for both the sender and the receiver. The end result has been that we are now reaching each other more quickly but not necessarily more effectively.

Most people prefer calling to writing because it takes less time. The American culture places a great deal of emphasis on accomplishing things as quickly and efficiently as possible. So, it is not startling[2] that we would place a ten-minute phone call to let a loved one know what is going on in our lives rather than spend an hour explaining details in a three-page letter. In addition, telephoning is more convenient because there is less work involved. When using the phone, we merely dial and begin to talk. At the end of the conversation, we hang up the receiver and the task is completed. When writing a letter, however, we must find stationery, write the letter, address it, get a stamp for it, mail it, and then wait who knows how long for a reply. Left to choose between the more expensive one-step telephone call and the cheaper multistep letter, the majority of us are willing to pay for the convenience of talking on the telephone.

A less obvious but equally important reason why people prefer using the telephone is that it is more immediately gratifying than a letter. A phone call gives a more complete picture of how each person is doing. One can pick up on[3] unspoken messages. During a telephone call one can, for example, tell whether the other person is angry, happy, nervous, or reticent.[4] This kind of information might be totally lost in a letter. Communicating over the telephone also feels more complete because it is spontaneous.[5] A two-way conversation is occurring. The speakers can discuss until they feel that they have understood each other. When I was in college, my parents would call me every Sunday afternoon so that my mother could hear for herself that I was "really OK." For her, my letters were informative, but she didn't feel we had truly made contact with each other until she could talk to me and hear my voice happily chattering in the receiver.

Because a telephone call is quicker and immediately gratifying, I'm afraid that we are beginning to forget the benefits of letter writing as a means of communication. A letter offers some advantages that a phone call does not. The writer can, for example, think carefully about what he wants to say. It gives him the chance to remember things he might forget in a spontaneous conversation. It also provides him with the time to organize his thoughts into a logical and comprehensible order. In other words, he has the luxury of saying exactly what he wants, the way he wants. In addition, a letter can be kept and enjoyed several times. Once a phone call is finished, however, you are left only with its memory. On lonely nights far away from home, rereading a few letters from family and friends can be very comforting.

In closing, our desire to give up letter writing for telephoning can be explained but should not be excused. Both phone calls and letters are effective means of getting in touch with loved ones far away from us. They just do it in different ways. Long-distance phone calls can never totally replace letters. If we lose the art of letter writing, we will lose part of our effectiveness to communicate with each other over long distances.

Vocabulary

[1]**to be summed up:** to be stated
[2]**startling:** surprising
[3]**to pick up on:** to notice
[4]**reticent:** shy, reserved
[5]**spontaneous:** automatic, natural

Discussion Questions

1. What are the basic ideas expressed in the introductory paragraph? Identify the thesis statement in this essay.

2. What is the purpose of this essay?

3. Where is the title of this composition? Would you consider this a good title or a weak one? Explain.

4. How many developing paragraphs does this essay have?

5. Does each paragraph play a role in developing or supporting the thesis statement? Explain.

6. As a group, do the paragraphs in this essay adequately develop the thesis statement? In other words, does this essay have unity? Explain.

7. How does the concluding paragraph let the reader know that the discussion is coming to a close? Does it restate the main idea of the essay? How?

8. After reading the entire essay, would you say that it has coherence? Explain.

EXERCISE 4: Distinguishing Between Strong and Weak Thesis Statements

The thesis statement of an essay, remember, presents the basic idea of the composition and explains the author's purpose for discussing the subject. Look at the following statements. Explain which of the following would be good thesis statements and which would not.

EXAMPLE: The United States makes many different types of cars to accommodate a variety of needs.

This is a weak thesis statement because it is so general. All the types of cars made in the United States cannot adequately be covered in one seven-paragraph essay. In addition, the thesis statement does not make clear what "different types" means. Does the writer plan to discuss how cars are different regarding their comfort, their ability to save gas, their power, or something else? It might be better to say, "One way to group cars made in the United States is to look at those that are fuel efficient with 'economy' comfort, those that are fuel efficient with 'luxury' comfort, and those that are fuel inefficient with luxury comfort. Each type has been designed to accommodate a population with a variety of needs."

EXAMPLE: Getting a driver's license in the United States is a simple process if you take the time to do each step completely and carefully. Basically, the process begins with learning your state's handbook of driving rules and regulations and ends with paying a fee so that you can receive your driver's license.

This is an example of a good thesis statement because it presents a specific idea—acquiring a driver's license in the United States—which can be covered well in one seven- to eight-paragraph essay. The thesis statement also gives the writer's point of view, namely, that getting a driver's license is easy if one follows each step completely and carefully. Finally, the writer briefly lets the reader know in this thesis statement that he or she is going to be explaining step by step how to get a driver's license by stating what the first and last steps are.

1. In my opinion, the Olympics should no longer be considered an international competition for amateur athletes. The athletes' access to deferred income from governments, private donations, and advertising promotions makes the title "amateur competition" a joke.

2. The Beatles wrote many songs with strong messages for their listeners.

3. The United States hopes to make great advances in its space program in the next decade.

4. People under the age of twenty-one should not be allowed to purchase alcohol. Three equally horrible accidents, each involving teenagers abusing alcohol, led me to believe this.

5. Cats and dogs are the two most popular pets in North American homes today. They have some characteristics in common that make them both good candidates for house pets. Yet these two animals are so strikingly different in their temperament and habits that one wonders how the North American public decided to accept both of them as their "favorite" pet.

6. A good writer of English should know the basic writing patterns.

7. Because of my fear of heights, there are three things I have tried but know I will never successfully do: parachute out of an airplane, climb a ladder over four feet off the ground, and jump off a high diving board into a pool.

8. Ms. Cunningham is one of the best teachers I have ever had.

EXERCISE 5: Writing Thesis Statements

The following statements are topics. They cannot be considered thesis statements for an essay because they do not contain at least one of the following: (1) a single idea; (2) a statement of the author's purpose for discussing the idea; (3) a brief introduction of the points that will be covered in the essay.

Try to turn these topics into good thesis statements.

EXAMPLE: How to paint a house well

In order to paint the exterior of a house well, one must have each of the following: adequate time to complete the job; sufficient patience to do the job carefully; good tools, including high-quality paint; and a great deal of stamina for the physically hard work.

1. Learning a first language is very different from learning a second language.

   _____

   _____

2. Body language can indicate anger or distrust of someone.

   _____

   _____

3. My three favorite kinds of music

   _____

   _____

4. Raising (or not raising) the speed limit of 55 mph on U.S. highways

   _____

   _____

5. The secondary education system in the United States versus the secondary education system in my country

   _____

   _____

EXERCISE 6: A Review of Important Terms in This Chapter

In this chapter you learned many new, important terms that you will be using throughout the rest of the book. Before you begin learning the basic writing patterns for the essay, let's review these terms.

Directions: Get into two teams. One person (who may be the instructor) will lead the game but not play. The leader picks one of the terms that follow (mixing up the order). The first player on each team then writes a definition for the term. Your instructor will decide which person wrote the best definition or explanation. That person will get a point for his or her team. Continue playing until all the terms have been defined. The team with the most points at the end wins the game. (*Note*: Depending on the quality of the responses, each time a word is defined the leader may want to give a point to each team, to only one team, or to neither team.)

Alternative Directions: Each student has a piece of paper numbered from one to fifteen. The instructor or students give definitions for each of the terms in random order. The students write down the name of each defined term. The student with the most correct answers at the end of the game wins.

Terms

short essay (composition)

writing strategies

paragraph

to indent

margin

topic sentence

developing sentences

conclusion

unity (for a paragraph or essay)

title

coherence (for a paragraph or essay)

introductory paragraph

thesis statement

developing paragraphs

author's purpose

2

Narration

Sometimes when you write, you want to tell a story. This is called *narration*. In narrative writing, you explain to others something that happened. When you tell friends about your trip from home to the United States, for example, you are using narration. Narration has three important qualities: (1) It tells a story, (2) it generally describes events in chronological order, and (3) it makes a point. Let's consider each one.

TELLING A STORY

Narration tells a story about a series of events or actions. The story can be fiction (not based on facts) or it can be nonfiction (based on real-life experiences). An example of fictional narration would be one about your travels from earth to the moon. An example of a nonfictional narration would be the written police report of an automobile accident you saw.

Whether your narration is fictional or nonfictional, it is important to choose verbs carefully. Verbs create the action in a story. Generally speaking, verbs should be in the active voice (he is sliding, she giggled, they were waiting) rather than in the passive voice (he was asked, she is given, they were sent away). Active verbs help keep your story moving and make the events seem more alive to your reader.

DESCRIBING IN CHRONOLOGICAL ORDER

Narrative details are ordered in a logical sequence of time. Usually the events are told in *chronological order*. This means that the story begins with what happened first and then explains the rest of the events in order, finishing with the one that happened last. Imagine, for example, that you wanted to tell a story about how you got a ticket late one night. You would probably tell the events in the following order:

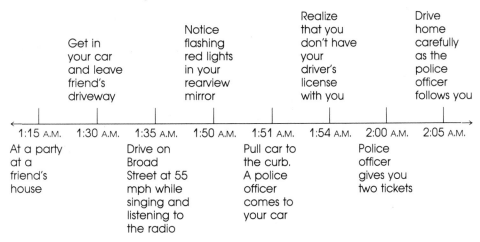

See how easy the story is to follow when you relate the events in order from 1:15 A.M. to 2:05 A.M.? What would happen if you mixed up this order? How would the story sound to your reader if, say, you explained what happened at 1:35 A.M., then told what occurred at 1:15 A.M., and finally stated what happened at 2:00 A.M.? Explaining events chronologically makes a story seem logical and easy to understand.

MAKING A POINT

You should have a purpose when writing a story. In other words, you describe events to teach something, persuade, or make a point. If you do not have a purpose, the reader will probably ask, "Why did I bother to read this?" In order to get your point across, it is important to select the correct details and to arrange them carefully. In any situation, a lot of details can be found. It is your job as the writer to emphasize the details that are significant to the point of the story and then omit the rest. Consider, for instance, the example about the speeding ticket. Every event listed on the time line leads to the point that if one gets caught driving too fast and without a license, he or she will probably get a ticket. Imagine that while this speeder was getting the ticket, two people in a passing car were discussing their plans for the next weekend. To mention this information in the speeder's story would be silly. You should make sure that every part of your story contributes in some way to the main point. If not, your reader may become bored or confused.

EXERCISE 1: Listing Events in Chronological Order

Get into groups of three. Read each pair of beginning and concluding sentences for a possible narrative story. In your group, list the major events or actions necessary for each story to go from the beginning sentence to the concluding one. Let your imagination go. The more detail you give, the better your story will be. When you finish, share your story with the others.

EXAMPLE: *(Beginning)*   I will never forget the morning I slipped on a piece of ice in front of the grocery store.

(Conclusion)   The doctor patted my leg and said, "In eight weeks your leg will be as good as new."

1. I fell flat on the ground and twisted my leg.

2. Several people rushed to help me get up.

3. I moaned as they put me into the taxi because my leg hurt so badly.

4. The taxi driver took me to the closest hospital, Research Medical Center.

5. The emergency room attendant made me wait two hours before I saw the doctor.

6. While I waited in the emergency room, I watched a rerun of "Dynasty" on a black-and-white television.

7. Finally, I had x-rays and learned that my leg was broken.

8. The doctor fixed the break and put on a cast from my ankle to my thigh.

9. I thought about how I had planned to go skiing next weekend.

10. I got very depressed and began to cry.

Sentences

Situation 1

(Beginning) When I opened the door to the darkened old house, I heard a chilling scream.

(Conclusion) I laughed when I thought about how scared I had been at hearing that woman's scream.

Situation 2

(Beginning) The dirty, unshaven man walked into the bank and slowly pulled out a loaded gun.

(Conclusion) The crowd outside on the street cheered as the police officers put the man into the police van.

Situation 3

(Beginning) "I can't believe this is happening on my very first plane flight," the young woman said to herself.

(Conclusion) As the plane touched the ground, she said, "I will *never* take a plane again as long as I live."

Situation 4

(Beginning) I bet that when John started digging in the back yard to plant his tomatoes, he never expected to find that shiny, hard object.

(Conclusion) The news reporter told John, "This isn't going to make you a rich man, but it sure is going to make you a famous one."

EXERCISE 2: Practice Making a Point When Writing a Narrative

Remember that when you write a story, it is important to have a purpose for doing so. This helps keep your reader interested in what you are saying. Generally you think of the point first and then make sure the events of the story support it.

Following are several possible topics for narratives. For practice, try to think of a point you could make for each one. When you finish, share your answers with the group. Notice how many different points you can make with one topic.

EXAMPLE

Topic: A story about the worst piano lesson of Michael's life

Point: It's not enough to have talent if you want to be a good piano player. You also have to be willing to practice hard every day.

1. *Topic:* What one international student did to get over his or her terrible homesickness

   Point: _____

   _____

2. *Topic:* A story about your constant attempt and failure to lose weight

   Point: _____

   _____

3. *Topic:* A story about the career of your favorite musician or musical group

   Point: _____

   _____

4. *Topic:* A story about your favorite relative or friend

   Point: _____

   _____

5. *Topic:* A story about a party you will always remember

   Point: _____

   _____

IMPORTANT VOCABULARY

The following words are commonly used when expressing thoughts in chronological order. These expressions will help you express the events in your narration in a logical order of time.

To Illustrate Time Sequence

At the beginning of your story you can use

In the beginning	*Example:*	*At first* I opened the door to go in, but my feet wouldn't move.
At first		
At the start		
First (of all)		

In the middle of your story you can use

Next	*Example:*	Katie knew that the *next* step she had to take was to call her parents.
After that		
Then		
Second, Third, and so on		
Following		
Subsequently		
Afterwards		
Meanwhile		

At the end of your story you can use

Eventually	*Example:*	Frank had *at last* learned the truth. He was going to be fired from his job tomorrow.
At last		
In conclusion		
Finally		
To sum up		
As has been noted		

To Illustrate Time Relationships (how one event relates to another in terms of time)

At the same time	*Examples:*	Carmen was working on the reports *while* Joyce was typing the last report.
During		

When

While

As

As soon as

Before

Until

After

Afterwards

The minute that

Before it gets cold again, I'm going to move to a better apartment.

I always open my junk mail *after* I open my bills.

Until her father helped her, Sara refused to ride down the escalator.

NOTE: The expressions illustrating time relationships are used in subordinate clauses (a subordinate clause is a part of a sentence expressing lesser facts and ideas). When the subordinate clause is at the beginning of the sentence, it is separated by a comma from the main clause (a main clause is a part of a sentence expressing the principle ideas). When the subordinate clause is at the end of the sentence, there is no comma separating it from the main clause. Look at the four sample sentences above as models.

To Point Out Specific Moments in Time

You can use prepositional phrases of time.

On April 20, 1980 (any date)

On Thursday (any day of the week)

At 6:30 A.M. (any exact moment in time)

At noon, night, midnight

In 1985 (any year)

In January (any month)

In the morning, afternoon, evening

In the summer, winter, fall, spring

EXAMPLES: *At noon*, the office will close for a lunch break.

On May 26, 1981, Alison was born.

In the fall, Steve gets hay fever very badly.

---

*EXERCISE 3: Practice Using Vocabulary
That Expresses Chronological Order*

A. Practice Vocabulary for Time Sequence. Form your chairs into a circle. You will take turns creating a six-line story. Person 1 will start the story using one of the "beginning" expressions on page xvi. Persons 2–5 will continue the story using one of the "middle" expressions on page xvi. Person 6 will finish the story using one of the "end" expressions on page xvi–xvii. Continue around the circle until everyone has had a chance to participate in making a story.

B. Practice Vocabulary for Time Relationships. Find a partner. Pick one of the expressions illustrating time relationships. Also choose two nouns to go with that expression of time. Tell them to your partner. He or she will make a sentence. Your partner can either write the sentence or say it. Take turns until you both have a chance to create four sentences.

EXAMPLES: Expression of time: *during*

    Noun: *chemistry test*

    Noun: *students*

    Sentence: One of the students was caught cheating during the chemistry test.

    Expression of time: *as soon as*

    Noun: *rain*

    Noun: *party*

    Sentence: As soon as the party began, it started to rain.

IMPORTANT PUNCTUATION/USAGE: Direct Speech

Often when you write a story, you want to use examples of *direct speech*. With direct speech, you repeat exactly the words of the speaker. The quoted words can come at the beginning or the end of the sentence. The quoted words can also be interrupted. Look at the examples here:

1. Teresa said, "Don't listen to Ellen. She likes to stretch the truth." (*quoted words at the end*)

2. "Why do I have to eat these awful vegetables?" Alison asked. (*quoted words at the beginning*)

3. "I don't want to swim," Ken moaned. "It's too cold today." (*quoted words interrupted*)

Regardless of which way you decide to quote words, it is important to pay special attention to the use of quotation marks and punctuation. Notice that the quotation marks go around the words the person is saying. If the speaker's words are interrupted, put quotation marks around each part of the quoted statement. Look at the examples here:

4. "I wish I could go fishing," Jamey said, "but I'd better fix this fence instead." (*one interrupted sentence*)

5. "Do I have to listen to that song again?" Adam asked. "I don't like it." (*two interrupted sentences*)

Commas, periods, and question marks that make up part of a quotation are put inside the quotation mark. Remember to put a final period, question mark, or exclamation point before the last quotation mark even if the quotation is only one-word or two-words long.

EXERCISE 4: Correct Use of Punctuation in Examples of Direct Speech

---

With your instructor, discuss each of the five quoted statements above. Where are the quotation marks? Where are the capital letters? Where are the commas, periods, and quotation marks in each statement? After looking at these, do you now understand how to use quotation marks and punctuation correctly in quoted statements? If not, ask your instructor for help.

EXERCISE 5: Practice Putting Correct Punctuation in Examples of Direct Speech

---

Practice putting quotation marks, punctuation, and capitalization in each of the quoted statements that follow. When you finish, show your instructor.

EXAMPLE: bill said don't wait up for me I'll be home late

Bill said, "Don't wait up for me. I'll be home late."

1. read the last two chapters in your book the instructor said

2. the secretary said please have a seat in the waiting room

3. do you want to see the new horror film Max asked

4. I can't decide which pair of shoes to buy Pat said

5. there aren't enough seats for me in this row Cyrus said maybe I'll just move to the last row

6. will you repeat the last line of that joke again asked Bonnie

7. Ann stated I'm not going to argue with you about that car anymore

8. please don't give me any more cake Margaret groaned I'm on a diet

EXERCISE 6: Practice Writing Your Own Direct Quotations

Ask five people in your class to make a statement or question for you. Write each one in direct quotation form. Use the examples as guides.

(quoted words at the beginning) *"I'll be glad when this class is finished,"*
Henry said.

(quoted words at the end) *Jerry asked, "Where do you want to go eat lunch?"*

(quoted words interrupted) *"I don't understand this assignment," Lisa said.*
"Can you help me?"

1. (quoted words at the beginning) _____

2. (quoted words at the end) _____

3. (quoted words interrupted) _____

4. (quoted words at the end) _____

5. (quoted words at the beginning) _____

GUIDED WRITING ACTIVITY

Have you ever wanted to create the ending to a story that you were reading or a television show that you were watching? In this writing activity, you are going to do just that. First, you are going to read the beginning to a story entitled "An Unforgettable Night in Nowhere." Then in small groups you are going to create your own ending for it.

Now, read the beginning of the story.

An Unforgettable Night in Nowhere

Something told me that I shouldn't have turned off the highway while driving alone at night. But John, now my ex–best friend, had said that this was the fastest way to get to the tiny airport in the next town. A few minutes ago it had started raining, and now it was coming down so hard that I could barely see the bumpy gravel road ahead of me. There were no lights, no cars, no people, just me in my 1972 Ford Pinto trying to catch the once-a-week flight back to the city. "How stupid can I be?" I wondered. "No plane is going to take off in weather like this anyway!"

All of a sudden there was a sharp streak of lightning that spread out like a large tree branch. A deafening burst of thunder followed it. Then the hail started coming down, pounding on the roof and hood of my car. I couldn't see anything out my front window.

I stopped the car and slumped back in my seat. Beads of clammy sweat rolled down my neck and back. "Now what am I going to do?" I groaned.

I tried to get out of the car to walk for help, but the strong winds pushed the door shut again. I was getting scared. No one really knew for sure where I was. I began to feel trapped.

Suddenly two lights in my rearview mirror caught my eye. They grew increasingly bigger and brighter as they approached my car. The lights stopped about three feet behind me. I didn't know whether to feel scared or relieved. My legs started to shake. I heard a door slam shut followed by the crunching sound of something walking on the wet gravel road. "What's going to happen now?" I asked myself.

You get to decide what happens next!

Peer Interaction

A. Get into groups of three or four.

B. Discuss the story so far. What is in the story? Where is the main character? What is happening? Is there anything you don't understand? If so, discuss it among yourselves until you understand.

C. Now as a group try to write the rest of the story. To begin, discuss the information you are going to use in the story.

STRATEGY FOR GATHERING INFORMATION

As a group, think of as many details as you can about the end of the story. Put the details in each category listed below. On a separate piece of paper, copy all the details. (See pages xiv–xv for information on using WH-questions.)

What happened?	*When and Where was it done?*	*Who did it?*
What happened to the person in the car?	Does the action take place in the car? outside the car? far away from the car?	Was it a man? a woman? a group of people?

How did he or she do it?	*Why did he or she do it?*
Specifically what steps did the person take to accomplish the major actions in the story?	What was the reason this event took place?

D. After you get all your details listed on the paper, discuss them. Do you understand each one? Do they seem to fit together? Should any details be eliminated because they are unnecessary? Should some details be added to make the events more complete? Ask your teacher for help if you'd like.

E. As a group, try to decide the purpose of this story. What point are you trying to make? Are you trying, for example, to show that it is dangerous to travel alone at night? Are you trying to show that when a person is in trouble, there is generally someone who will help? Are you trying to make some other point? Once you decide the purpose of your story, write it here:

Purpose: _____

_____

F. As a group, try to put the main events of the rest of the story in a logical order. Briefly list the events on a piece of paper.

G. Look at the vocabulary list on pages 23 and 24 of the text. Do you see any vocabulary terms for chronological order that could be used with your sentences in activity F? Make note of which words you might use and where they should go.

H. Do you feel that you are ready to begin working on a draft of the story? If not review steps B through G until you feel ready to begin writing. Each person in the group will write his or her own ending to the story based on the information you have gathered.

Organizing Your Information

1. Now think about the information you have gathered for your story. Also think about your purpose for the story.

2. Try to organize this information into a clear, concise narration. Read the entire outline given here before you begin.

3. This outline is a suggestion to get you started. Narration does not generally follow the exact format of the essay outlined in chapter one. It does not, for example, have to have a definite introduction or a thesis statement. It is, however, still important to pay attention to paragraphing, coherence, and unity. If you would like to organize your story differently than suggested here, discuss your idea with your teacher and then go ahead.

Paragraph One: Your Beginning to the Rest of the Story

In this paragraph, explain what happens in the story immediately after the main character asks, "What's going to happen now?" Use the information you have gathered as a group to guide you. Be sure to use active verb tenses and vivid details to make the events come alive for your reader.

What is your topic sentence for this paragraph? Write it here:

_____

_____

What important information should be in this paragraph? Write it here:

_____

_____

_____

Are you going to use any expressions of chronological order in this paragraph? Note them here:

_____

Paragraph Two: The Next Major Event in the Story

In this paragraph, describe the next major event in the story. Follow the directions outlined in paragraph one.

What is the topic sentence for this paragraph? Write it here:

_____

_____

What important information should be in this paragraph? Write it here:

_____

_____

_____

Are you going to use any expressions of chronological order in this paragraph? Note them here:

_____

Paragraph Three: The Following Major Event in the Story

In this paragraph, describe the following major event in the story. Follow the directions outlined in paragraph one.

What is the topic sentence for this paragraph? Write it here:

_____

_____

What important information should be in this paragraph? Write it here:

_____

_____

_____

Are you going to use any expressions of chronological order in this paragraph? Note them here:

_____

Following the pattern just outlined, include as many paragraphs as necessary to detail the rest of the major events in your story.

Last Paragraph: The Conclusion to Your Story

In the last paragraph, bring the events of your story to a logical end. Be sure that you have answered the following questions: What was done in the story? When and where was it done? Who did it? How did he or she do it? Why did he or she do it? This would also be a good place to include the purpose of your story. It can be stated directly or indirectly. It can be stated seriously or humorously.

What is the topic sentence for this paragraph? Write it here:

_____

_____

What important information should be in this paragraph? Write it here:

_____

_____

_____

How are you going to express the purpose of your paper? Write it here:

_____

_____

Are you going to use any expressions of chronological order in this paragraph? Note them here:

_____

Rough Draft

Now using your notes, write the first draft of your composition.

Peer Editing

Find a partner and exchange your compositions. Follow these steps:

1. Read your partner's composition. Do not make any marks on the paper the first time you read it. Just try to get the main point.

2. Reread the paper. Underline any words, phrases, or expressions that don't seem correct or that are difficult to understand.

3. Do you have any questions about the content of the composition? If so, write them on the Comments Sheet.

4. Now write three suggestions to the writer for improving his or her composition.

5. Give the composition and Comments Sheet to your partner.

Writing Your Final Draft

First consider the points from your partner's Comments Sheet. Add them to your rough draft if needed. Then write the final draft of your composition.

Questions to Ask Yourself before Handing in Your Paper

Put a check mark in each box after you complete the tasks.

☐ Do the paragraphs clearly present the points I am trying to make?

☐ Does each paragraph have enough information so that the reader can understand what I am saying?

☐ Have I used chronological-order vocabulary terms to help one idea flow smoothly into the next?

☐ Are the words spelled correctly? Are my verbs in the active voice? Did I punctuate my direct speech sentences correctly?

When you finish your composition, give it to your instructor. After your instructor evaluates your composition, discuss it with him or her.

> NOTE: With this particular assignment, it might be fun to read your composition to the whole class. Notice how many different kinds of endings people have created for the same story.

ADDITIONAL NARRATION TOPICS

1. Write about the scariest experience you have ever had.

2. Write about the first time you traveled somewhere without your family.

3. Write about how you met your girlfriend or boyfriend, fiancé or fiancée, or husband or wife.

4. Write about a time in which your "less than perfect" English skills got you into an embarrassing, funny, or frustrating situation.

5. Write a mystery story in which something very valuable is stolen. In the

story have three people who could have committed the crime. Finish your story by explaining which one really did it.

6. Write a story about ghosts. Your purpose in writing the story is to frighten your reader.

7. Write about one experience in which you caused someone unhappiness or sorrow. Explain what you learned from that experience.

3

Description

Generally when you write, you want to describe your subject very clearly. When finished reading the description, the reader should be able to see the subject in his or her mind as clearly as you see it in yours. Imagine, for example, that you wanted to describe your parents to a new friend. In your mind you have a very clear picture of your parents, including the soft lines around your father's eyes and the happy chuckle of your mother's laugh. Your friend, however, has no past images of your parents. He or she must rely on your words. Your goal, then, is to use enough carefully chosen, specific details in your description so that your friend could pick your parents out of a group of people.

When describing a subject, one can use two kinds of details: *objective* details and *subjective* details. Objective details are those that describe factual information about the subject based on the five senses (sight, touch, taste, smell, and hearing). There is no emotion or opinion in objective details. In contrast, subjective details are those that express the reader's personal opinion on the subject. The details do not have to be based on factual information. Look at the following descriptive details of a movie theater five minutes before the movie begins. If you have trouble understanding why a certain detail is objective or subjective, ask your instructor. Can you add a few details to each list?

Objective Details	*Subjective Details*
red velvet-covered seats	the nauseating smell of stale candy, salted popcorn, and cigarette smoke
torn golden curtains	
light-pink walls covered with fingerprints and chewed gum	bumpy seat cushions that feel as if they belong in a 1920 Ford
a red-and-gold rug with the letters *BB* stamped on it	the ice-cold stare of a child mad at his parents
crumpled paper cups and spilled popcorn on the floor	the usher walking toward the screaming children like an army sergeant
	the buzzing sound of the audience

Here are a few suggestions to help you when using description:

1. Don't try to describe everything about a subject. You will end up with much information and your reader will become lost trying to sort it all out. Rather, choose one single impression or idea and have all your details focus on that. Imagine, for example, that you wanted to show that an airport, even with all its activity, is a very lonely place. All your details would help to describe the loneliness.

2. Once you gather all your subjective and objective details for your subject, decide which ones will effectively help you describe it. Keep those that will help you; eliminate those that won't.

3. Choose descriptive details that distinguish your subject from others like it. If you are describing your Siamese cat, for example, emphasize those features that make it different from other Siamese cats.

4. Remember to describe your subject using all the senses: hearing, touch, taste, smell, and sight. Too often we describe something only in terms of how we see it because sight is the strongest sense. This, however, gives a one-dimensional quality to the description. Your readers do not just want to know what a hamburger looks like. They want to know how it feels, smells, and tastes when a person bites into it.

It is important to mention that in educational and business situations, you will probably not write a great number of purely descriptive essays. Description is used a great deal, however, in combination with some of the writing patterns you are going to learn (with classification and comparison and contrast, for example). For this reason, it is important to learn how to use description effectively.

ORGANIZING THE DETAILS
IN A DESCRIPTIVE ESSAY

One way to organize the information in a descriptive essay is to use *spatial order*. Using spatial order means putting the details in a logical arrangement of space or location. This logical arrangement can describe details in a variety of ways:

from left to right or from right to left

from top to bottom or from bottom to top

from front to back or from back to front

from the center to the outside or the outside to the center

If, for example, you were going to describe yourself, you would probably start at the top, with your head, and work your way down to your toes. If you were going to describe your classroom, you might want to start at the front of the room and describe the details in order to the back of the room. Take a few minutes as a class to decide how you might most effectively describe each of the following:

- a soccer or football stadium
- a hospital room
- a statue or monument in your city
- your brother's or sister's face
- a computer
- a new highway being built

EXERCISE 1: Practice Writing Descriptive Sentences

Following are several nouns. Think of what descriptive vocabulary could be added to each noun to create a vivid picture. First write down the descriptive vocabulary. Then write a good sentence or two using it. Look at the example here:

> **EXAMPLE:** car (yellow, Buick, dented, 1980, convertible, no radio antenna)
>
> *In college my car was a yellow 1980 convertible Buick. It had a big dent on the right rear fender and the radio was missing.*

1. tree (*details:*   )

   _____

   _____

2. girl (*details:*   )

   _____

   _____

3. bridge (*details:*   )

   _____

   _____

4. hands (*details:*   )

   _____

   _____

5. boat (*details:*   )

   _____

   _____

6. pants (*details:*   )

_____

_____

7. song (*details:*   )

_____

_____

EXERCISE 2: Practice Creating and Identifying Subjective and Objective Descriptive Details

Individually, for each of the topics that follow, make lists of subjective and objective details similar to the ones made earlier about the movie theater. Then get into pairs. Take turns reading your descriptive details for each topic. Your partner will decide whether the details are subjective or objective. If there is a question, discuss it until you agree upon the answer or ask your instructor for help.

1. The inside of an airplane

2. A doctor's waiting room

3. Your best friend

4. A police car

5. Your table at dinner

IMPORTANT VOCABULARY

The following words and phrases are commonly used when expressing thoughts in spatial order. These expressions will help you express the events in your descriptive essay in a logical order of space or location. Review their meaning with your instructor.

To face
To be opposite
On, at, in
Under, beneath
Over, on top of
At the top of, on the side of, at the bottom of

Inside, outside

Beside, next to, near, in between

In back of, in the middle of, in front of

(To) (on) the left (of), (to) (on) the right (of)

Across from

(At) (on) the corner of

At the end of

EXAMPLES

- The church *faces* a library and a museum on Brighton Avenue.
- A small door is *at the top of* the monkey's cage.
- A nonbreakable window is *on the side of* the cage.
- A heavy metal floor is *at the bottom of* the cage.
- The students were sitting *in front of* their teacher in the auditorium.
- The teacher sat *in back of* the students so that he could watch them.
- Nick's Beauty Shop is located *at the corner of* Fifty-sixth Street and Broadway Avenue.

EXERCISE 3: Practicing Spatial-Order Vocabulary

On a separate piece of paper, write several sentences describing each of the following subjects using spatial order. Try to use the vocabulary you have just learned. Remember that we can describe details from

left to right or right to left

top to bottom or bottom to top

front to back or back to front

the center to the outside or the outside to the center

EXAMPLE: Describe your kitchen.

The kitchen is in the shape of a rectangle. On the left, when you first walk in, is the sink. To the right of the sink is a big counter. Below the sink and the counter is a row of large cabinets. Next to the big counter is the refrigerator. Across from the refrigerator is a deep storage closet. To the right of the closet is another smaller counter. Next to the counter is the stove. Above the counter and the stove is a row of small cabinets. On the right, next to the stove, is the doorway out of the kitchen.

Topics

1. Describe the arrangement of your classroom.

2. Describe a classmate or your instructor.

3. Describe one of your favorite pictures or photographs.

4. Describe your face.

5. Describe the inside of your car (or the inside of a bus, subway, or taxi).

For extra practice: Once you describe the topic spatially, go back and add objective and subjective details to make the description more interesting.

IMPORTANT PUNCTUATION/USAGE: The Fragment and the Run-On

In English there are two kinds of sentence patterns you want to avoid: the *fragment* and the *run-on*.

The Fragment

The fragment is an incomplete sentence written as though it were complete. In other words, the sentence does not have a complete thought; a part of the sentence is missing. Following are several examples of fragments followed by correct forms of the sentence. If you do not understand the corrections, please ask your instructor to explain them. There is more than one way to correct a sentence fragment. If you can think of other ways to correct these fragments, share them with the class.

Incorrect: Listens to the music with his eyes closed.

Correct: John listens to the music with his eyes closed.

Incorrect: Ben hit his hand on the counter. *And gave us the meanest look we had ever seen.*

Correct: Ben hit his hand on the counter and gave us the meanest look we had ever seen.

Incorrect: I was really bored. *Waiting for the train to arrive.*

Correct: I was really bored waiting for the train to arrive.

Incorrect: This being the only time I could make the appointment.

Correct: This was the only time I could make the appointment.

Incorrect:	I don't like vegetables. *Especially spinach.*
Correct:	I don't like vegetables, especially spinach.
Incorrect:	Doctors believe there are several factors that can cause cancer. *For example, your diet, your exposure to certain chemicals, and your family history.*
Correct:	Doctors believe there are several factors that can cause cancer. For example, many doctors believe that your diet, your exposure to certain chemicals, and your family history can influence whether or not you will get cancer.
Incorrect:	Because Karen didn't want to go.
Correct:	Because Karen didn't want to go, she pretended that she was sick.
Incorrect:	Before the movie ended.
Correct:	We left the theater before the movie ended.

The Run-On

The run-on has two or more complete sentences punctuated as if they were one sentence. In other words, the run-on sentence has two subjects and two verbs that express two complete thoughts, but the two thoughts are not separated correctly. Below are several examples of run-ons followed by correct forms of the sentences. If you do not understand the corrections, ask your instructor to explain them. There is more than one way to correct a run-on sentence. If you can think of other ways to correct each run-on, share them with the class.

Incorrect:	The mountains were beautiful we didn't want to leave.
Correct:	The mountains were beautiful. We didn't want to leave.
Incorrect:	My advisor told me to take Calculus I next semester she said I need to take it for my major.
Correct:	My advisor told me to take Calculus I next semester; she said I need to take it for my major.
Incorrect:	I just learned my parents want me to come home next summer, why didn't they tell me when I talked to them two nights ago?
Correct:	I just learned my parents want me to come home next summer. Why didn't they tell me when I talked to them two nights ago?
Incorrect:	The play began at 7:30 P.M., it finished at 10:15 P.M.
Correct:	The play began at 7:30 P.M., and it finished at 10:15 P.M.
Incorrect:	My aunt is an elderly woman she is afraid to live alone.
Correct:	My aunt is an elderly woman; she is afraid to live alone.

Incorrect: The lawyer didn't think he could help the young man he said he would try to help anyway.

Correct: The lawyer didn't think he could help the young man, but he said he would try to help anyway.

Incorrect: Tomorrow we're going to have a big test, it's going to be on run-ons and fragments.

Correct: Tomorrow we're going to have a big test. It's going to be on run-ons and fragments.

EXERCISE 4: Correcting Run-Ons and Fragments

Some of the following sentences are run-ons, some are fragments, and still others are correct. Read each sentence carefully. Identify each one as run-on (R-O), fragment (FRAG), or correct (C). Change the run-ons and fragments into good sentences.

EXAMPLES	**SENTENCE TYPE**
Unless he has enough money.	*FRAG*
Henry won't move unless he has enough money to get a much bigger place.	
The president made a twenty-minute speech afterwards the reporters asked him questions.	*R-O*
The president made a twenty-minute speech. Afterwards the reporters asked him questions.	

1. Being the only choice she had in this situation.

   _____

   _____

2. While he waited for the test to begin.

   _____

   _____

3. There are many places to buy that kind of wine I know of two stores.

   _____

   _____

4. I improved my grade in this class several different ways. In-   _____
   cluding studying more for tests and reading the textbook carefully.

   _____

   _____

5. It's not difficult to learn how to work with a computer if you   _____
   can follow directions and have a lot of patience.

   _____

   _____

6. Mary had a big decision to make she wanted to be alone.   _____

   _____

   _____

7. Jerry got very scared. And ran to hide behind the parked cars.   _____

   _____

   _____

8. The police officers walked up to the door on the count of three,   _____
   they pushed it open, and carefully walked inside.

   _____

   _____

9. Waiting for TOEFL test results is a nervous experience.   _____

   _____

   _____

10. Listening to the other people's conversation.   _____

    _____

    _____

11. My father prefers reading fiction. While my mother likes reading   _____
    nonfiction.

    _____

    _____

12. A very skilled man. Mr. Johnson has been practicing his profes-   _____
    sion for thirty-five years.

13. Mrs. Thompson has several medical problems. Including dia-   _____
    betes and asthma.

14. The dealer has too many new cars, their prices are going to have   _____
    to be lowered very soon.

15. The fire department was called to a big fire three buildings were   _____
    already burning when they arrived.

16. While I was at the museum, I got to see a mummy for the first   _____
    time in my life.

17. While I listened to the professor's lecture.   _____

18. The young lady was arrested for her crime; she couldn't believe   _____
    she had been caught.

19. Susan cannot stand to be near roses. Being allergic to them.   _____

20. Three marine biologists are studying the dirty ocean water the   _____
    local residents want to clean it up.

21. Marie completed her English studies very quickly. After she _____
became a serious student.

_____

_____

22. Some people get nervous when they drink strong coffee, it doesn't _____
bother me at all.

_____

_____

23. Especially young children and the elderly. They shouldn't spend _____
a lot of time in the heat.

_____

_____

24. Miguel just graduated from the university now he is going to _____
return to his country.

_____

_____

25. She didn't want to take world history she liked it once she took _____
it though.

_____

_____

GUIDED WRITING ACTIVITY

When you go to the cinema to watch a movie, do you ever notice what the movie theater is like five minutes before the show begins? There are lots of different sights, sounds, and smells. They combine together to form an interesting picture. In this essay you are going to have a chance to give your description of a movie theater five minutes before the show begins.

Peer Interaction

A. First, obviously, you need to go to a movie. Get there at least fifteen minutes early so that you have time to observe the room and the people. If possible it might be fun to go to the movies with some of your classmates.

B. STRATEGY FOR GATHERING INFORMATION

At the theater take some notes of what you find. Take a piece of paper with you that is organized like this:

Things you can

SEE	HEAR	TOUCH	SMELL	TASTE

Make notes of the theater and the people there as you observe them (see pages xiii–xiv for observing). You don't have to use perfect English or think carefully about your ideas. Just think of an idea and then write it down. Try to write down both *objective* and *subjective* details.

C. The next time you have class, separate into groups of three. Share your lists of information with each other. Can you begin to see certain details that might be grouped together?

D. You will probably not want to use all the information you have gathered in your lists. Can you begin to see which pieces of information you want to use and which you don't? Can you think of any other descriptive details to add that could help your description of the movie theater? Ask your teacher for help if you'd like.

E. Now try to decide on a purpose for this description. What point are you trying to make by describing a movie theater five minutes before the movie begins? Are you trying, for example, to show that there are certain sights, smells, and sounds which are at all movie theaters before the movie begins? Are you trying to make some other point? Once you decide on the purpose of your essay, write it here.

Purpose: _____

_____

F. Discuss each other's purposes. Do they seem logical and worth mentioning? Is each writer's purpose easy to understand? Is there anything he or she could do to improve it?

G. Now take a few minutes to explain briefly to each other how you plan to describe the movie theater. Try to think of two or three major observations you plan to make about the theater and the people there. You might tell the others in your group, for example, that you plan to describe the movie theater in terms of what you notice most: the food, the noises, and the audience. Listen carefully to each other's brief descriptions. If you have any helpful comments to make, give them to each other.

H. Do you feel you are ready to begin working on a draft of your description? If not, review steps C through G until you feel you are ready to begin writing.

Organizing Your Information

1. Now think about the information you have gathered for your description of the movie. Also think about your purpose for describing the movie theater.

2. Try to organize this information into a clear, concise description. Read the entire outline before you begin.

3. This outline is a suggestion to get you started. Description does not generally follow the exact format of the essay outlined in chapter one. It does not have to have a definite introduction or a thesis statement, for instance. It is still important, however, to pay attention to paragraphing, coherence, and unity. If you would like to organize your description differently to suit your needs better, discuss your idea with your teacher and then go ahead.

Paragraph One: The Beginning of Your Description

In this paragraph let the reader know that you are describing a movie theater five minutes before a movie begins. Try to give specific details so that the description will come alive for your reader. You might want to mention, for example, the name and location of the theater, the time you attended, and the name of the film you saw. You might also want to mention your purpose in describing a movie theater five minutes before the show begins.

What is your topic sentence for this paragraph? Write it here:

_____

_____

What important information should be in this paragraph? Write it here:

_____

_____

Are you going to use any expressions of spatial order in this paragraph? Note them here:

_____

_____

Paragraph Two: Your First Major Observation of the Theater

What is the topic sentence for this paragraph? Write it here:

_____

_____

What important information should be in this paragraph? Write it here:

_____

_____

Are you going to use any expressions of spatial order in this paragraph? Note them here:

_____

_____

Paragraph Three: Your Second Major Observation of the Theater

What is your topic sentence for this paragraph? Write it here:

_____

_____

What important information should be in this paragraph? Write it here:

_____

_____

Are you going to use any expressions of spatial order? Note them here:

_____

_____

Paragraph Four: Your Third Major Observation of the Theater

What is your topic sentence for this paragraph? Write it here:

_____

_____

What important information should be in this paragraph? Write it here:

_____

_____

Are you going to use any expressions of spatial order? Note them here:

_____

_____

Paragraph Five: The Conclusion to Your Description

In the last paragraph, bring your description of the movie theater to an end. Also try to make an interesting observation. You might, for example, want to mention that all the sights, sounds, and smells of the theater combined to make a "living painting." What interesting point would you like to add? Write it here:

_____

_____

What is your topic sentence for this paragraph? Write it here:

_____

_____

What important information should be in this paragraph? Write it here:

_____

_____

Are you going to use any expressions of spatial order? Note them here:

_____

_____

Rough Draft

Now using your notes, write the first draft of your composition.

Peer Editing

Find a partner and exchange your compositions. Follow these steps:

1. Read your partner's composition. Do not make any marks on the paper the first time you read it. Just try to get the main point.

2. Reread the paper. Underline any words, phrases, or expressions that don't seem correct or that are difficult to understand.

3. Do you have any questions about the contents of the composition? If so, write them on the Comments Sheet.

4. Now write three suggestions to the writer for improving his or her composition.

5. Give the composition and Comments Sheet to your partner.

Writing Your Final Draft

First consider the points from your partner's Comments Sheet. Put them into your rough draft if needed. Then write the final draft of your composition.

Questions to Ask Yourself before Handing in Your Paper

Put a check mark in each box after you complete the tasks.

☐ Do the body paragraphs clearly present the points I am trying to make?

☐ Does each paragraph have enough information so that the reader can understand what I am saying?

☐ Have I used spatial-order vocabulary to help one idea flow smoothly into the next?

☐ Are the words spelled correctly? Did I eliminate all fragment and run-on sentences?

When you finish your composition, give it to your instructor. After your instructor evaluates your composition, discuss it with him or her.

ADDITIONAL DESCRIPTION TOPICS

1. Describe a person not in your family who made a very strong impression on you.

2. Describe the photograph at the beginning of this chapter. Imagine that the person for whom you are describing this picture has no idea what it is.

3. Describe a part of your personality that is least understood by others. Give a lot of detail about that part of your personality.

4. Describe your favorite restaurant or store in the city in which you are now living. Remember to use both subjective and objective details.

5. Describe a place where you can go to be alone and relax.

6. Describe something (a type of building, store, restaurant, appliance, and so on) in North America that doesn't exist in your country. In your description let the reader know why this place or thing seemed so strange or unusual to you.

7. Describe your "dream car." Remember to use both subjective and objective details.

4

Illustration

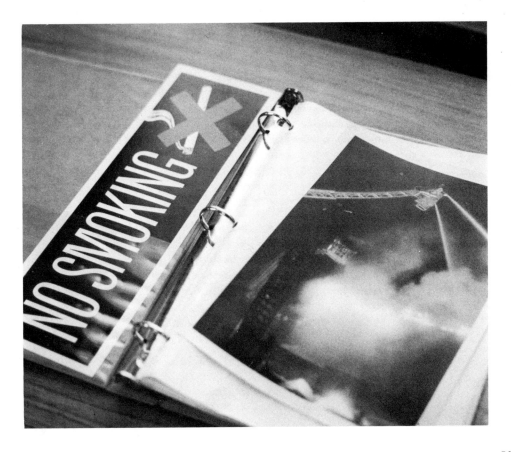

Often when you write a paper, you want to make a point and then support it with specific information. This is called *illustration*. The point that you make is general. In other words, it is a statement that is widely accepted to be true or correct. It can also be a personal opinion that you have about a certain subject. Look at the following examples of general statements:

- On the whole the ages of thirteen to nineteen are difficult for both the teenagers themselves and for their parents.
- Generally speaking, Americans are trying to cut down on the amount of salt, sugar, and fat they eat in order to protect their health.
- A student must have a strong background in the basic skills if he or she expects to succeed in college or the university.

While these statements may generally be held to be true, in a piece of writing they are considered weak or not credible if the writer does not develop them more fully. For this reason a good writer will *support, prove,* or *explain* the general idea through the use of carefully developed specific statements. These specific statements can be examples, statistics, facts, or details. Look at the following specific statements:

- On the whole the ages of thirteen through nineteen are difficult both for the teenagers themselves and for their parents. *As an example, my sister, who is now a lawyer and a mother of three, ran away from home four times during her teenage years. My parents even had to get her out of jail when she was just fifteen!* (specific support through an example)
- Generally speaking, in order to protect their health Americans are trying to cut down on the amount of salt, sugar, and fat they eat. *Long-term medical studies run in Massachusetts, California, and Texas have shown that these three factors increase the risk for such serious illnesses as heart disease and high blood pressure.* (specific support through facts)
- A student must have a strong background in the basic skills if he or she expects to succeed in college or the university. *For example, at Bryant College only 15 percent of the students reading below the tenth-grade level did passing work in their first history class. In contrast, 82 percent of those students reading above the tenth-grade level did passing work in this course.* (specific support through statistics)
- The minute I walked in the front door, I knew I was in trouble. *The icy stare of my parents, the rigid posture of my school counselor, and the downcast eyes of my little sister* told me that this was not going to be a pleasant encounter. (specific support through details)

Illustration **55**

By supporting your general idea with strong specific statements, you help clarify the point you are trying to make. In addition, you give credibility to your ideas. If you do a good job specifically explaining your general idea, the reader of your paper should be able to say, "Yes, I understand exactly the point the writer is trying to make."

ORGANIZING THE SPECIFIC POINTS IN AN ILLUSTRATION

When illustrating a general idea, you can use three different ways to organize the specific points:

1. The specific points can have equal importance.

2. The specific points can be listed from the least to the most important.

3. The specific points can be listed from the most to the least important.

The following paragraph has been organized in each of these three ways.

Specific Points Having Equal Importance

I like my job! In fact, there are several reasons why I am happy to work as an accountant. *First*, I get the chance to do what I trained so long for. *Second*, I earn money to pay my living expenses. *Finally, and equally as important*, I work because it gives me a sense of belonging to a group that shares my professional ideas and interests. The people with whom I work offer a kind of companionship that I cannot find with family or other friends.

Specific Points Listed from the Least to the Most Important

I like my job! In fact, there are several reasons why I am happy to be an accountant. *First*, I work at an accounting firm because it gives me a sense of belonging to a group of individuals who share my professional ideas and interests. These people offer a kind of companionship that I cannot find with family or other friends. *Also*, my job gives me a great deal of professional fulfillment. I get the chance to do what I trained so long for. *Finally and most important*, I am an accountant because it lets me earn enough money to pay my living expenses. If I didn't earn enough money to live on, I couldn't keep the job regardless of how much professional fulfillment or companionship it offered.

Specific Points Listed from the Most to the Least Important

I like my job! In fact, there are several reasons why I am happy to be an accountant. *First and most important*, I am an accountant because I need to earn money to pay my living expenses. If the job didn't pay enough money to pay my living expenses, I couldn't consider keeping it. My job *also* gives me a great deal of professional fulfillment. I get the chance to do what I trained so long for. *Also worth mentioning* is that I work because it gives me a sense of belonging to a group that shares my professional ideas and interests. The people with whom I work offer a kind of companionship I cannot find with family or other friends.

So, you have some choices in how to present the specific points that support your general idea. You can decide that each point is equal in importance and then list the points in any order you wish. You can also decide that certain points have more importance than others. In this latter case, you can present the most important point first to make a strong first impression and then follow it by other, less important points. Or, you can present the less important points first, building up to a strong conclusion by finishing with the most important point.

EXERCISE 1: Distinguishing Between General and Specific Statements

---

Look at the following statements. Decide if each one is expressing a general idea or a specific one. Discuss your answers together.

_____ 1. Oranges, grapefruit, and lemons are all examples of fruit that grow well in this type of climate.

_____ 2. The latest report shows that there was only a 2 percent increase in the number of bad checks written last year. This year, however, there was a 25 percent increase. These statistics are alarming.

_____ 3. As a rule, people who are studying to be engineers must take many math courses.

_____ 4. It is well known that one must meet certain requirements in order to rent an apartment in this complex.

_____ 5. For instance, a person must learn how to insert a diskette properly before operating a personal computer.

_____ 6. As an illustration, Mrs. Baker refused to shop in that grocery store after the robbery occurred.

Illustration **57**

_____ 7. Paying income taxes in the United States is generally considered a complicated process.

EXERCISE 2: Creating Specific Examples for General Statements

---

Following are five general statements. Think of several specific statements that could support, prove, or explain each one. List these specific points under each general statement. For extra practice decide how these specific points should be presented and then put them in order. For example, should they be written from the most to the least important? from the least to the most important? Share your work with the group.

EXAMPLE

Instructors use much more than books to teach English.

a. For example, they often use VCRs and televisions to give students practice listening to commercials, parts of movies, video music, and so on.

b. Another way teachers have students practice listening comprehension is with tape recorders that can play songs, lectures, conversations, and pre-recorded English lessons.

c. Teachers also use computers to give students a chance to practice grammar and vocabulary lessons at their own pace.

d. Another example is the use of magazines and newspapers in the classroom to give students practice reading about current events.

1. There are several "tricks" one can use to do well on a test.

   a.
   b.
   c.
   d.

2. One of the best ways to learn is by one's mistakes.

   a.
   b.
   c.
   d.

3. The clothes that I wear reflect my personality.

   a.
   b.

c.

d.

4. The human body, if not properly protected from the natural elements (extreme cold, heat, the sun, and so on) can suffer serious injury.

a.

b.

c.

d.

5. When I am sitting in a dentist's chair waiting for the dentist to come, everything I see reminds me of pain.

a.

b.

c.

d.

IMPORTANT VOCABULARY

The following words and phrases are commonly used when expressing a general idea.

Generally (speaking)
In general
On the whole
For the most part
As a rule
It is widely accepted that

EXAMPLES

As a rule, airplane pilots must have a great deal of actual flying experience before they are allowed to work for a commercial airline.

On the whole, the TOEFL test is considered to be one reliable indicator of an ESL student's readiness to begin college-level courses.

The following words and phrases are commonly used when expressing a specific idea.

Illustration **59**

Namely

For example

For instance

In particular

As an (another) example

As an (another) illustration

Specifically

That is

To illustrate

To show

To prove

To be examples of

EXAMPLES

Specifically 47 percent of the school's budget came from tuition while 9 percent came from private gifts.

"I Love Lucy" and "Star Trek" *are two examples of* old television programs that are as popular today as when they were first shown.

The following words and phrases are commonly used to point out one idea in a paper as being more important than other ideas mentioned:

The most important
                interesting
                critical
                unusual
                illuminating

The strongest
     greatest
     biggest
     best
     worst

Above all

Especially

Most important

EXAMPLES

There were many reasons why I decided to sell my car. *The most important reason*, however, was that the transmission was going bad.

Of course, many things about this little girl fascinated me. What I found to be *the most interesting* was that she could already speak three languages fluently at the age of six.

My doctor suggested that I exercise. *Above all*, he said that I have to lose twenty pounds by the end of the summer.

EXERCISE 3: Practicing Illustration Vocabulary

Get into groups of four or five. Look at the list of topics that follows. One person will start by making a general statement about one of the subjects. The next three people in the group will each make a specific point to support it. If you think that your specific point is the most important, then use one of the appropriate vocabulary phrases when stating it. Continue until your group has gone over all of the subjects. If you have time, write down your sentences and share them with the class.

EXAMPLE: credit cards

Person 1:   Generally speaking, when people use credit cards they spend too much money.

Person 2:   For example, when you buy something with a credit card, you have to pay interest on that purchase — sometimes as much as 21 percent annually.

Person 3:   As another example, I know that I buy more items with a credit card than when I write a check because it doesn't seem as if I'm really paying for them.

Person 4:   Also, I will go to an expensive restaurant when I use my credit card but to a cheap fastfood place when I pay with cash. This illustrates that credit cards tend to encourage people to go to places where they would have to spend more money.

Topics

1. current movies

2. cars

3. violence in big cities

4. living alone (without one's family)

5. keeping cool during hot weather

Illustration **61**

IMPORTANT PUNCTUATION/USAGE: Simple Sentences and Compound Sentences

Simple Sentences

To give variety to our writing, we use several different types of sentence patterns. The first sentence pattern you probably learned is the *simple sentence*. The simple sentence is made up of one subject-verb group that expresses one idea. Here are some examples of simple sentences. Can you identify the subject and the verb?

The thief ran.

Howard always plays soccer on Thursday.

We don't have enough money to pay for the accident.

Sometimes simple sentences have more than one subject. Look at the following examples. Can you find the subjects and the verb in each one?

Susan and Bill met at the museum.

The ice and the snow formed a deadly combination on the highway.

Sometimes simple sentences have more than one verb. Look at the following examples. Can you find the subject and the verbs in each one?

Karen washed and dried her laundry last night.

The car violently jerked and then stopped.

Sometimes simple sentences have many subjects and verbs. Look at the following examples. Can you find the subjects and verbs in each one?

The waitress and the busboy took the order, served the dinner, and cleaned the table together.

The doctor, the nurse, and the patient discussed the patient's illness, made plans for his surgery, and set a date for his release from the hospital.

So you see that simple sentences can be very short or quite long. The important thing to remember is that the simple sentence expresses one idea regardless of its length or its number of subjects and verbs.

Compound Sentences

The compound sentence contains two complete simple sentences that are usually joined together by a comma and a connecting word like *and, but, for, or, nor, so,* or *yet.* There are two important points to remember about the compound sentence pattern:

1. Both ideas in the sentence are considered equally important.
2. The two ideas are related to each other in meaning.

Look at the following examples of the compound sentence:

Elizabeth wants to go to college after high school, *but* Brian wants to find a job.

We can eat the pizza at the restaurant, *or* we can take it home.

Mike didn't study his vocabulary words last night, *so* he did very poorly on the quiz this morning.

Watch out! When you combine two simple negative sentences using *nor*, the grammatical structure of the compound sentence can be tricky. Look at the following examples and ask your instructor to explain them if you don't understand.

I didn't wash my car this afternoon, *nor did I go* to the grocery store.

Joe doesn't like to play golf, *nor does Al* like to play football.

The government won't raise the taxes this year, *nor will it eliminate* any present social programs.

EXERCISE 4: Practice Making Simple Sentences

Create simple sentences following the guidelines in parentheses.

EXAMPLE: (one subject, two verbs)

The little girl cried softly and wiped her eyes from time to time.

1. (one subject, one verb) _____

_____

2. (one subject, one verb) _____

_____

3. (two subjects, one verb) _____

_____

Illustration **63**

4. (one subject, three verbs) _____

_____

5. (two subjects, one verb) _____

_____

EXERCISE 5: Practice Making Compound Sentences

Combine the following simple sentences into good compound sentences using a comma and one of the following connecting words: *and*, *but*, *so*, and *or*. Be sure your sentences make sense.

EXAMPLE: We wanted to paint the kitchen.

Jim couldn't find the bucket of paint.

We wanted to paint the kitchen, but Jim couldn't find the bucket of paint.

1. My sister brought a tossed salad to the party. I brought a jello salad.

_____

_____

2. The flood waters reached the edge of the shopping center. They didn't do any damage.

_____

_____

3. I couldn't decide which course to take. I asked my counselor for her advice.

_____

_____

4. The dealer said the car cost 8,000 dollars. His competitor would sell it for much less.

_____

_____

5. Next year I can visit my grandparents in Australia. Next year I can visit my best friend in Canada.

_____

_____

6. Create your own compound sentence using *and*.

_____

_____

7. Create your own compound sentence using *but*.

_____

_____

8. Create your own compound sentence using *so*.

_____

_____

9. Create your own compound sentence using *or*.

_____

_____

10. Create your own compound sentence using *nor*.

_____

_____

GUIDED WRITING ACTIVITY

In English there is the saying "Rules are made to be broken." By this we mean that there are situations when it is acceptable, even necessary, to break a certain rule. Can you think of times when you or someone you know made the *right* decision by breaking a rule? In this writing activity you are going to show through several specific examples why different rules should sometimes not be followed or obeyed.

Peer Interaction

A. Get into groups of three or four.

B. STRATEGY FOR GATHERING INFORMATION

As a group, for about ten minutes, you are going to make a list (see page xiii for listmaking) about different examples of when people have broken a rule. You are also going to examine why each rule was broken. Try to think of as many different examples as you can.

Illustration **65**

Rule That Was Broken	**Why It Was Broken**

C. Now take a few minutes to look at your group's list. Of course, you will not want to use all the examples the group came up with. Can you begin to see which three or four examples you would most like to use to support your paper? Try to narrow the list down to the three or four strongest examples.

D. Take a few minutes to think carefully about each example.

E. Now get together as a group again and explain in detail each example you plan to use in your paper to show that there are times when rules are meant to be broken. Evaluate each other's explanations. Do they seem complete and interesting? Do they also explain why the writer felt it was right not to follow the rule in this particular situation? Can you think of any information to add? Help each other create strong explanations of each example. Also ask your teacher for help if you'd like.

F. Do you feel you are ready to begin working on a draft of your illustration? If not, review steps A through E until you feel you are ready to begin writing.

Organizing Your Information

1. Now think about the information you have gathered for your three or four examples. Also think about how these examples prove the point of your paper, namely, that in certain circumstances it is acceptable, even necessary, to break a rule.

2. Try to organize this information into a clear, concise illustration. Read the entire outline given here before you begin.

3. This outline is a suggestion to get you started. If you would like to organize your composition differently, discuss your idea with your teacher and then go ahead.

Paragraph One: Introduction to Your Illustration

In this paragraph briefly introduce the idea that you believe there are situations when it is permissible to break a rule. Remember that showing this is actually the purpose of your paper. Let the reader know you are going to illustrate this idea through several specific examples. You might or might not want to mention specifically what the rules are or why it was necessary to break them. Don't give a lot of detail. In the introduction, you just want to present the main idea to your reader.

What important information should be in your introduction? Write it here:

_____

_____

What is your thesis statement? Write it here:

_____

_____

Are you going to use any expressions for illustration in this paragraph? Note them here:

_____

_____

Paragraph Two: The First Example to Support Your Illustration

NOTE: Think about how you are going to present your examples. Are they all going to be equally important? If not, are you going to present the most important example first? Are you going to present it last?

What is your topic sentence for this paragraph? Write it here:

_____

_____

What important information should be in this paragraph? Write it here:

_____

_____

Did you remember to explain both which rule was broken and why?

Illustration **67**

Are you going to use any expressions for illustration in this paragraph? Note them here:

_____

_____

Paragraph Three: The Second Example to Support Your Illustration

What is your topic sentence for this paragraph? Write it here:

_____

_____

What important information should be in this paragraph? Write it here:

_____

_____

Did you remember to explain both which rule was broken and why?

Are you going to use any expressions for illustration in this paragraph? Note them here:

_____

_____

Paragraph Four: The Third Example to Support Your Illustration

What is your topic sentence for this paragraph? Write it here:

_____

_____

What important information should be in this paragraph? Write it here:

_____

_____

Did you remember to explain both which rule was broken and why?

Are you going to use any expressions for illustration in this paragraph? Note them here:

_____

_____

Paragraph Five: The Conclusion

In the last paragraph, bring the information of your three examples to an end. Also try to make an interesting observation. You might have noticed, for example, that all three examples were about rules that were broken for the same reason. Perhaps you observed that it was all right to break these three particular rules because they hurt rather than helped people. What interesting point would you like to add?

What is the topic sentence for this paragraph? Write it here:

_____

_____

What important information should be in this paragraph? Write it here:

_____

_____

Are you going to use any expressions for illustration? Note them here:

_____

_____

Rough Draft

Now using your notes, write the first draft of your composition.

Peer Editing

Find a partner and exchange your compositions. Follow these steps:

1. Read your partner's composition. Do not make any marks on the paper the first time you read it. Just try to get the main point.

2. Reread the paper. Underline any words, phrases, or expressions that don't seem correct or are difficult to understand.

3. Do you have any questions about the contents of the composition? If so, write them on the Comments Sheet.

4. Now write three suggestions to the writer for improving his or her composition.

5. Give the composition and Comments Sheet to your partner.

Illustration **69**

Writing Your Final Draft

First consider the points from your partner's Comments Sheet. Add them to your rough draft if needed. Then write the final draft of your composition.

Questions to Ask Yourself Before Handing In Your Paper

Put a check mark in each box after you complete the tasks.

☐ Do I have a clear introduction with a good thesis statement?

☐ Do the paragraphs clearly present the points I am trying to make?

☐ Does each paragraph have enough information so that the reader can understand what I am saying?

☐ Have I used expressions showing general to specific order to help one idea flow smoothly into another?

☐ Do I have a variety of simple and compound sentences?

When you finish your composition, give it to your instructor. After your instructor evaluates your composition, discuss it with him or her.

ADDITIONAL ILLUSTRATION TOPICS

1. Pick one type of nonverbal communication (body language) and show through specific examples how it can convey clear and strong messages without words. Ask your instructor to explain body language if you are unsure what it means. Consider using one of the following types of body language:

   the eyes

   touching

   use of arms and legs

   distance

2. Show through specific examples that some of our greatest inventions were thought of because we really *needed* them at the time, not just because somebody wanted them. Explain what the inventions are and why we needed them. You might want to consider these:

   the telephone

   the telegraph

   the personal computer

the automobile

the radio

3. Show through specific examples that television commercials do not always present their products as they really are.

4. Show through specific examples that our pets sometimes understand us and communicate with us as well or better than do people.

5. Show through specific examples that people often buy more expensive items just because of the name or status and not because they are necessarily better than cheaper and less famous brands. Consider brands of watches, jeans, cars, certain foods, and so on.

6. There is a saying that it is more fun to give gifts than to receive them. Do you agree with this? Why do you think it is so? In this essay, give either several specific examples or one long extended example illustrating that a person receives much joy by giving to others.

7. Pick any proverb from your culture and show through specific examples that the proverb is true. Here are some examples of proverbs that might help you get started. Ask your teacher to explain them if you do not understand.

"All good things must come to an end."

"In every dark cloud there is a silver lining."

"Do not put all your eggs in one basket."

"The early bird catches the worm."

"An ounce of prevention is worth a pound of cure."

5

Instructional Process

Sometimes when you write a paper, you want to give a set of directions explaining how to do something. You might, for example, want to explain how to roast a chicken or how to change the oil in your car. When you state step by step how to do something, you are providing an *instructional process*.

An important point to remember is that your set of directions should be clear and easy to follow. If another person cannot understand your directions, there is really no point to writing them. Here are some suggestions to help you write clear, easy-to-follow directions:

a. Make each step of the directions as simple as possible. Remember that you are trying to instruct, not confuse, your reader.

b. Be sure to include every necessary step. If you leave out an important step, your directions won't work. Imagine, for example, that you are explaining to your readers how to downhill ski. If you forget to tell them when and how to fasten their boots and skis, they may not do it properly and as a result suffer serious injury to their ankles or feet.

c. Remember to put your steps in chronological order. In other words, list the steps in the exact order in which they happen (First, . . . Next, . . . After that, . . .). If necessary, review the information you learned about chronological order in chapter two.

d. Be sure to tell your readers about any special equipment or materials they might need in order to complete this set of directions. In addition, if the materials or equipment are new vocabulary words for your readers, be sure to define them. Suppose, for example, that you were explaining how to bake a cheesecake. In addition to identifying the ingredients needed to bake the cake, let your readers know that they need a *springform pan*. This is a pan used for baking cheesecakes that has detachable sides fastened to the bottom by a clamp or a spring.

IMPORTANT USAGE AND IMPORTANT VOCABULARY: Expressions of Time, Repetition of Key Words, and Pronoun Reference

When writing an instructional-process paper, it is very important to make clear that you are going from one step to the next. Here are three ways that we do this:

1. By using expressions of time

2. By repeating important words and phrases

3. By using pronoun reference

Let's look at each way individually.

Expressions of Time

One way to show that you are moving from step to step is to use the expressions of time that you learned in chapter two. There are some other expressions of time that help you link one step to the next. Here are a few:

Expressions for Actions Happening at the Same Time

While, as, the minute that, when
At the same time, meanwhile

EXAMPLES

While he is dieting, he is exercising every day.
He is exercising every day *while* he is dieting.

Mary is learning English; *at the same time*, she is taking typing.
Mary is learning English. *At the same time*, she is taking typing.

Expressions for Actions Happening One after the Other

When, after, before, until
Afterwards, then, following that

After George cut his hand on the broken glass, he had to get stitches in it.
George had to get stitches in his hand *after* he cut it on the broken glass.

Barbara will finish her bachelor's degree next May; *following that*, she will begin working on her master's degree.
Barbara will finish her bachelor's degree next May. *Following that*, she will begin working on her master's degree.

Repetition of Important Words and Phrases

A second way to show your readers that you are going from one step to the next in your process paper is to repeat key words or phrases several times throughout the essay. This gives a feeling of continuity to your ideas. Look at the following paragraph. Notice which words are repeated: *frostbite, step, warm, victim.* Why are these particular words mentioned several times?

Treating Frostbite

Injury to a part of one's body from exposure to extreme cold is called *frostbite*. The parts of the body that are hurt by frostbite are generally quite small: the nose, cheeks, ears, fingers, and toes. One should follow several *steps* when treating a *victim* of frostbite. The first step one should follow is to cover the frozen part of the body. In the next step one should give the victim extra clothing and blankets to help him or her warm up. Third, bring the victim indoors as soon as possible. Then give him or her a warm drink. The most important step is to rewarm the frozen part quickly by putting it in warm, but not hot, water. This allows the frozen part of the body to warm up slowly. The last step in the treatment of frostbite should be to get medical help for the victim as soon as possible.

Pronoun Reference

A third way to show your reader that you are going from one step to the next in your process paper is to use pronoun reference. This means simply that you first write a word and then repeat it later in the sentence or essay in pronoun form. Like the repetition of important words, pronoun reference gives a feeling of continuity and unity to your ideas. Look at the following sample sentences:

I wanted John to keep the flowers, but he gave them to his mother instead.

In order to get an I-20 from our school, you must ask for an application and an Affidavit of Support form. Once you receive these papers, you fill them out and mail them back to us.

Practice Process Paragraph

The following instructional process paragraph makes use of expressions of time, repetition, and pronoun reference to help clearly explain the different steps in opening a checking account. Read the paragraph carefully and then answer the questions following it.

1   Opening a checking account at a bank is a fairly simple process if you understand the different steps involved. The first step is to find a bank that is convenient and provides the specific banking services you need. The next step is to
5   sit down with a bank officer to discuss which type of checking account is best for the kind of deposits you will make. For example, he or she can open one for you that doesn't give interest and doesn't require a minimum balance. Or, you can

have one that gives interest but requires a daily balance of

10 five hundred to a thousand dollars. The third step is to
complete a checking account application. It will generally
ask you basic questions about such things as your place of
employment, your home address, and your social security
number. As soon as you do this, you will make your first

15 deposit into your new checking account. It can be made
either in cash or by check. The step after this one is fun.
At this point you get to pick out which color and style
checks you want. They can be blue, yellow, pink, or green.
Most banks even have some with a picture printed on them.

20 Now comes the last step. You have to wait until this first
deposit in your checking account clears (is available
to you). After it has cleared, you can begin to write checks!

Discussion Questions

1. How many expressions of time can you find?

2. Which important words are repeated several times throughout the composition? Why did the writer use these particular words several times?

3. In line 7 to what does "he or she" refer?

   In line 7 to what does "one" refer?

   In line 9 to what does "one" refer?

   In line 11 to what does "it" refer?

   In line 14 to what does "this" refer?

   In line 15 to what does "it" refer?

   In line 16 to what does "this one" refer?

   In line 18 to what does "they" refer?

   In line 19 to what does "some" refer?

   In line 20 to what does "this" refer?

   In line 22 to what does "it" refer?

EXERCISE 1: Practice Using Expressions of Time

Use each group of words to create interesting sentences. Share your work with the class.

EXAMPLE: Until, movies, dinner

You can't go to the movies with Roger until you finish your

dinner!

1. while, the snow, wind

2. before, the exam, the football game

3. afterwards, the doctor, the patient

4. at the same time, the little boy, the little girl

5. as, the police officer, the stalled car

6. following that, the good news, the bad news

7. when, Joe, Jack

EXERCISE 2: Practice Using Pronoun Reference and Expressions of Time

---

Following is a short paragraph explaining how to cook American-style fried chicken. It sounds wordy because there is no pronoun reference. This means that the writer used the same words several times in a row without switching to their pronoun forms. The paragraph is also a little difficult to follow because the writer forgot to use any expressions of time to show that the process is moving from one step to the next. To improve the paragraph, follow these directions:

a. Rewrite the paragraph.

b. Change words to their pronoun form where appropriate.

c. Also add some expressions of time to make the paragraph sound better.

d. Share your rewritten paragraph with the group.

Fried chicken is one of the most popular foods in North America. Anyone can learn to make it well if he or she just follows these few simple steps. Cut the chicken into pieces. Wash all the chicken pieces in cold water. Cover the chicken pieces with flour, salt, and pepper. Get a big frying pan. Put a little salad oil in the frying pan. Heat the frying pan to 375 degrees. Add the chicken pieces to the frying pan. Brown the chicken pieces on all sides by cooking the chicken pieces for about twenty minutes. Remove the chicken pieces from the frying pan. Drain almost all the oil from the frying pan. Put the chicken pieces back in the frying pan. Reduce the heat to low. Cook the chicken pieces covered for about thirty minutes. Cook the chicken pieces uncovered for about ten minutes until the chicken pieces are crisp and tender. Serve the chicken pieces immediately on a heated platter.

EXERCISE 3: Practice Finding Key Words for a Process Essay

Remember that one way to bring unity to a process paper is to repeat important words throughout the essay. In this exercise you are going to practice selecting key words for process essays. Following are several topics. Get into groups of three or four. Together for each topic decide on three or four key words that you think would be good to repeat if you were writing an essay about it. Share your words with the class.

1. The steps necessary to take good care of yourself when you have a cold or flu

2. The steps necessary for a successful job interview

3. The steps necessary to change a tire

4. The steps necessary to prepare boiled rice

5. The steps necessary to get enrolled at your school

6. The steps necessary to take a good photograph

7. The steps necessary to make your home safe from robbery

GUIDED WRITING ACTIVITY

One thing that many international students want to get soon after they arrive in North America is a driver's license. Imagine that a friend from your country is going to study in your city next semester. In an essay, explain step by step how to get a driver's license where you now live. Begin with the first step of picking up the state book of driving laws and end with the last step of receiving your actual driver's license.

Peer Interaction

A. Get into groups of three or four

B–1. STRATEGY FOR GATHERING INFORMATION IF YOU DON'T KNOW HOW TO GET A DRIVER'S LICENSE

If no one in your group has gotten a driver's license, it would be a good idea for each of you to interview at least one American who has a driver's license (see page xiii for interviewing). Ask that person to give you the steps to getting a driver's license. Write all the steps as he or she tells them to you.

Before you finish check with the American to make sure you have all the information he or she wanted to give you.

B–2. STRATEGY FOR GATHERING INFORMATION IF YOU KNOW HOW TO GET A DRIVER'S LICENSE

As a group, for about fifteen or twenty minutes you are going to make a list of all the steps necessary to getting a driver's license (see page xiii for listmaking). Don't worry about getting the steps in order at this point. Just try to think of all the important things you need to do and write them down.

C. Look at your group's list. If you each have a separate list, combine them into just one. Now try to put the steps in order. Number them if this will help.

D. Look at the list again. Does it seem as if any steps are missing? If so, add them to the list in the correct order. Ask your teacher for help if you'd like.

E. Now think of a few key words that should be repeated throughout your essay. Also think of several expressions of time you could use to help link one step to the next. Write them down. Ask your teacher for help if you'd like.

F. Next, try to decide on the purpose of your paper. What point are you trying to make by explaining the different steps necessary in getting a driver's license? Are you trying to show, for example, that your state makes it intentionally difficult to get a driver's license? Are you trying to show that it's easy to get a license if you follow all the necessary steps but very difficult if you don't? What point are you trying to make? Write it here:

_____

G. Discuss each other's purposes. Do they seem logical and worth mentioning? Is each writer's purpose easy to understand? Is there anything he or she could do to improve it?

H. Do you feel you are ready to begin working on a draft of your process paper? If not, review steps A through G until you feel you can begin writing.

Organizing Your Information

1. Now think about the different steps you have gathered to explain how to get a driver's license in the city where you are now living. Also think about your purpose for writing the paper.

2. Try to organize this information into a clear, concise essay. Read the entire outline given here before you begin.

3. This outline is a suggestion to get you started. If you would like to modify it to suit your needs better, discuss your idea with your teacher and then go ahead.

Paragraph One: Introduction to the Process of Getting a Driver's License

Briefly introduce the idea that in order to get a driver's license in North America, it is necessary to follow a series of steps. Mention that in this paper you are going to explain this process step by step. If you'd like, mention what the first and last steps are. Don't give a lot of detail. In the introduction you just want to present the main idea.

What important information should be in the introduction? Write it here:

_____

_____

What is your thesis statement? Write it here:

_____

_____

Paragraph Two through Paragraph ??: The Steps for Getting a Driver's License

In the body paragraphs you are going to explain step by step how to get a driver's license in the city where you are now living. You should decide how you want to organize the information. You might want each step, for example, to be explained in a separate paragraph using a lot of detailed information. Or you may find that several steps should be combined together into one paragraph by a strong topic sentence. Ask your teacher for help if you are having difficulty organizing the material. For each paragraph, answer the following questions:

What is your topic sentence for this paragraph? Write it here:

_____

_____

What important information should be in this paragraph? Write it here:

_____

_____

Are you going to use any expressions of time or key words? Note them here:

_____

_____

Last Paragraph: The Conclusion

In your conclusion bring the information from your introduction and body paragraphs together. In addition, try to add an interesting point. You might, for example, want to comment on a particular step in the process that seems silly or unnecessary. What interesting point would you like to add?

What is your topic sentence? Write it here:

_____

_____

What important information should be in this paragraph? Write it here:

_____

_____

Are you going to use any expressions of time or key words? Note them here:

_____

_____

What interesting point are you going to add to your conclusion? Write it here:

_____

_____

Rough Draft

Now using your notes, write the first draft of your composition.

Peer Editing

Find a partner and exchange your compositions. Follow these steps:

1. Read your partner's composition. Do not make any marks on the paper the first time you read it. Just try to get the main point.

2. Reread the paper. Underline any words, phrases, or expressions that don't seem correct or that are difficult to understand.

3. Do you have any questions about the contents of the composition? If so, write them on the Comments Sheet.

4. Now write three suggestions to the writer for improving his or her composition.

5. Give the composition and Comments Sheet to your partner.

Writing Your Final Draft

First consider the points from your partner's Comments Sheet. Put them into your rough draft if needed. Then write the final draft of your composition.

Questions to Ask Yourself before Handing in Your Paper

Put a check mark in each box after you complete the tasks.

☐ Do I have a clear introduction with a good thesis statement?

☐ Do the paragraphs clearly present the points I am trying to make?

☐ Does each paragraph have enough information so that the reader can understand what I am saying?

☐ Have I used repetition of key words, pronoun reference, and time expressions to help one idea flow smoothly into the next?

☐ Are the words spelled correctly?

When you finish your composition, give it to your instructor. After your instructor evaluates your composition, discuss it with him or her.

ADDITIONAL INSTRUCTIONAL-PROCESS TOPICS

1. Imagine that something where you live needs to be repaired. Explain step by step how to do it.

2. Explain step by step how to have a successful job interview. Consider what you need to do before, during, and after the actual interview.

3. Explain step by step how a computer works. (You could also explain how a microwave oven, a television, a radio, a doorbell, or a lightbulb works.)

4. Explain step by step how solar heating warms a building.

5. Explain step by step how to perform cardiopulmonary resuscitation (more commonly called CPR) for a person who has stopped breathing.

6. Explain step by step how to prepare a very popular traditional dish from your country.

7. Explain step by step how to build a fire in a fireplace or outside at a campfire.

6

Classification

Sometimes when you write a paper, you want to separate one large topic of similar ideas or items into distinct categories. Suppose, for example, that you wanted to organize the topic "Hotels in My City." You might want to categorize them by their cost:

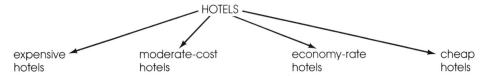

expensive hotels | moderate-cost hotels | economy-rate hotels | cheap hotels

The benefit of classification is that it allows you to take what otherwise would be an unwieldy topic for any essay and then separate it into manageable parts. Imagine, for example, that you started to write an essay about the students in your English program. You would probably soon find that you couldn't present all the different students in a logical manner unless you first *grouped* them into smaller categories of students sharing similar qualities.

A large topic can be classified in a variety of ways. Think again about the topic "Hotels in My City." You could classify hotels in a variety of ways:

expensive, moderate cost, economy rate, cheap (cost)

luxurious, above average, average, "fleabag" (quality)

close to downtown, close to highway, close to airport (accessibility)

The way you organize your topic depends on the point you are trying to make or the purpose of your essay.

EXERCISE 1: Categorizing Topics for Different Purposes

Look at the following general topics. Think of at least two different ways you could categorize each topic depending on the point you want to make.

EXAMPLE: Sports

1. *individual, pairs, team* (purpose: *number of players*)

2. *high risk, average risk, low risk* (purpose: *amount of danger*)

Topics

A. Friends

_____

_____

B. Books

_____

_____

C. Cars

_____

_____

D. Music

_____

_____

E. Vegetables

_____

_____

EXERCISE 2: Distinguishing Between Good and Poor Classification Topics

Look at the following statements. Decide if each one is or is not an example of classification. Explain your answers.

Yes/No

_____ 1. Steaks can be grouped as those that are cooked rare, medium rare, medium, medium well, and well done.

_____ 2. Restaurants fall into the categories of McDonald's, Shoney's, and Trader Vic's.

_____ 3. American movies can be classified as funny and scary.

_____ 4. Food can be categorized into the four basic groups: proteins, fruits and vegetables, starches, and dairy products.

_____ 5. Holidays in the United States are organized into those that are Christian and those that are government sponsored.

IMPORTANT VOCABULARY

The following words and phrases are commonly used in a classification paper:

Verbs

To sort, to be sorted (into)

To divide, to be divided (into)

To classify, to be classified (into)

To categorize, to be categorized (into)

To group, to be grouped (into)

To organize, to be organized (into)

EXAMPLES: The United States categorizes postsecondary educational institutions into vocational and technical schools, community colleges, four-year colleges, and universities.

Postsecondary educational institutions in the United States are categorized into vocational and technical schools, community colleges, four-year colleges, and universities.

Nouns

Sorts

Divisions

Classes

Categories

Groups

Types

Kinds

Aspects

Qualities

Characteristics

EXAMPLES: There are, generally speaking, two kinds of weather in Caracas, Venezuela: mild and rainy and mild and dry.

There are three kinds of music that I particularly enjoy: jazz, rock and roll, and classical.

EXERCISE 3: Practicing Classification Vocabulary

Find a partner. Choose a word or phrase from the preceding list. Your partner will identify it as either a verb or a noun. He or she will make a good classification statement using that word. Repeat until you both have a chance to make several sentences. Ask your teacher or an English speaker if you don't understand how to use any of the vocabulary items.

IMPORTANT PUNCTUATION: The Colon in a Series and the Comma in a Series

Here are some punctuation rules that are worth noting before writing a classification paper.

A. The Colon in a Series. The colon (:) is often used to introduce a series of items at the end of an independent clause.

EXAMPLES

When I go hiking, there are five things I always have with me: sturdy shoes, thick socks, fresh water, high-energy food, and a good compass.

The essay generally has three basic parts: the introductory paragraph, the developing paragraphs, and the concluding paragraph.

B. The Comma in a Series. The comma (,) is used between words, phrases, or clauses in a series. The items in the series must all be parallel in construction. This means that if the first item in a series is a noun, the other items must also be nouns. If the first item is a past perfect verb form, then the others must also be past perfect verb forms, and so on.

EXAMPLES

My younger brother will read only *travel digests, sports magazines,* and *comic strips.*

I'm ashamed to admit that I have *cheated, stolen,* and *bribed* to get what I want.

Alison felt *angry, confused,* and *lonely* as she stood waiting in the middle of the restaurant.

EXERCISE 4: Practice Using the Colon

Write five sentences using the colon to introduce a series.

EXAMPLE: In Adler and Towne's interpersonal communication text, three styles of solving arguments are presented: win-lose, lose-lose, and no-lose.

1. _____

2. _____

3. _____

4. _____

5. _____

EXERCISE 5: Practice Using the Comma in a Series

Write four sentences using the comma in a series. The form of the items you should use are given in parentheses.

> **EXAMPLE**: (verbs) I *hired, trained,* and *fired* the new employee all on the same day.

1. (nouns) _____

_____

2. (verbs) _____

_____

3. (noun phrase) _____

_____

4. (adjectives) _____

_____

GUIDED WRITING ACTIVITY

In North America there are many different types of family units. There is, for example, the traditional family with a married couple and their children living together. There is also the one-parent family where children live with either their mother or father, but not both. One can also find couples who marry and decide never to have children. Can you think of other types of families that you have seen or heard about in the United States?

Peer Interaction

A. Get into groups of three or four.

B. STRATEGY FOR GATHERING INFORMATION

As a group, for about ten to fifteen minutes, you are going to make a list of every type of family unit you can think of (see page xiii for listmaking). Really stretch your imagination. Be sure you can identify exactly who is a part of each family unit (natural parents and children, one stepparent and one natural parent with children, and so on).

LIST

Family Unit	*Its Members*
Traditional family	Natural mother, natural father, children

C. Now take a few minutes alone and look at your group's list of families. Are there reasons why you decided to classify families this way? Try to decide on a purpose for your classification of families. What point are you trying to make by grouping families this way? Are you, for example, trying to make the point that strong families can have two natural parents, one natural parent, or no natural parents? Take a few minutes to think of what point you are trying to make. Write the point here.

Purpose: _____

_____

D. Discuss each other's purposes. Do they seem logical and worth mentioning? Is each writer's purpose easy to understand? Is there anything he or she can do to improve it?

E. Once you have decided on your purpose, look again at your list from step B. Is the list too long or not well organized for your needs? Should any of the families be listed as parts of a larger or broader family unit? For example, did you list divorced mothers and fathers with children and unwed mothers and fathers with children as two separate categories? Would it be better to combine them under a more general category of one-parent families with children? Reorganize the list in step B so that you get the three or four categories of families that are most helpful for your composition.

F. ANOTHER STRATEGY FOR GATHERING INFORMATION

Once you decide on the different categories for your classification, you need to gather some information about each one. To do this you are going to take a few minutes to brainstorm about each category (see page xii for brainstorming). Form your ideas about each type of family and write them down.

YOUR CLASSIFICATION OF FAMILIES

First Category	Second Category	Third Category

G. Now take a few minutes to share with each other your information for each category. Evaluate each other's lists of information. Do they seem complete? Are there interesting details? Can you think of any other information to add? Help each other create strong lists for each category. Also ask your teacher for help if you'd like.

H. Do you feel you are ready to begin working on a draft of your classification paper? If not, review steps A through G until you feel you can begin writing.

Organizing Your Information

1. Now think about the information you have gathered on your categories of families. Also think about your justification, or purpose, for classifying them this way.

2. Try to organize this information into a clear, concise essay. Read the entire outline given here before you begin.

3. This outline is a suggestion to get you started. If you would like to modify it to suit your needs better, discuss your idea with your teacher and then go ahead.

Paragraph One: Introduction to Your Classification of Family Units

Briefly introduce the idea that families in North America are constructed, or categorized, in many ways. Explain how you have classified the different types of American families. Also explain your purpose or reasoning in grouping families in this particular manner. What point are you trying to make? Don't give lots of detail. In the introduction, you just want to present the main idea to your reader.

What important information should be in your introduction? Write it here:

_____

_____

What is your thesis statement? Write it here:

_____

_____

Are you going to use any vocabulary expressions for classification? Note them here:

_____

_____

Paragraph Two: First Category of Families

What is your topic sentence for this paragraph? Write it here:

_____

_____

What important information should be mentioned about this category? Write it here:

_____

_____

Are you going to use any vocabulary expressions for classification? Note them here:

_____

_____

Paragraph Three: Second Category of Families

What is your topic sentence for this paragraph? Write it here:

_____

_____

What important information should be mentioned about this category? Write it here:

_____

_____

Are you going to use any vocabulary expressions for classification? Note them here:

_____

_____

Paragraph Four: Third Category of Families

What is your topic sentence for this paragraph? Write it here:

_____

_____

What important information should be mentioned about this category? Write it here:

_____

_____

Are you going to use any vocabulary expressions for classification? Note them here:

_____

_____

Paragraph Five: The Conclusion

In your conclusion bring the information from your introduction and body paragraphs together. In addition, try to add an interesting point. You might want to mention how startlingly different these family units are from those in your country. You might want to mention one impact these different families have made on U.S. society in your opinion. What interesting point would you like to add?

What is your topic sentence for this paragraph? Write it here:

_____

_____

What important information should be mentioned about this category? Write it here:

_____

Rough Draft

Now using your notes, write the first draft of your composition.

Peer Editing

Find a partner and exchange your compositions. Follow these steps:

1. Read your partner's composition. Do not make any marks on the paper the first time you read it. Just try to get the main point.

2. Reread the paper. Underline any words, phrases, or expressions that don't seem correct or that are difficult to understand.

3. Do you have any questions about the contents of the composition? If so, write them on the Comments Sheet.

4. Now write three suggestions to the writer for improving his or her composition. Give the composition and Comments Sheet to your partner.

Writing Your Final Draft

First consider the points from your partner's Comments Sheet. Add them to your rough draft if needed. Then write the final draft of your composition.

Questions to Ask Yourself before Handing in Your Paper

Put a check mark in each box after you complete the tasks.

☐ Do I have a clear introduction with a good thesis statement?

☐ Do the paragraphs clearly present the points I am trying to make?

☐ Have I used classification vocabulary so that the reader can understand what I am saying?

☐ Did I use the comma and the colon correctly in my sentences that introduce a series of items?

When you finish your composition, give it to your instructor. After your instructor evaluates your composition, discuss it with him or her.

ADDITIONAL CLASSIFICATION TOPICS

1. Organize and discuss the types of friends you have.

2. Classify the types of books or magazines you read. If you prefer, classify the types of films you go to or the kinds of television shows you watch.

3. Categorize the types of crimes committed in your society or in North American society.

4. Group the different kinds of places you have lived in during your lifetime. (This is a particularly interesting composition if you have lived in several places that differ from each other.)

5. Classify the types of music you like or don't like to listen to. Discuss why.

6. Classify the types of politicians or government leaders in your country. You could sort the politicians or government leaders in North America if this would be more interesting to you.

7. Group the types of recreational activities you participate in here in North America (or at home).

7

Cause and Effect

Sometimes when you write a paper, you want to explain why something happened (*cause*) or what the consequences (results) were of something happening (*effects*). This is called a *cause-and-effect* paper. You might, for example, want to discuss the three reasons why you were hired for a job you really wanted (the causes). You might also want to mention the consequences this had on your personal life (the effects).

ORGANIZING A CAUSE-AND-EFFECT PAPER

You can write a paper that discusses only causes or only effects. Generally speaking, however, both cause(s) and effect(s) are presented in an essay. A cause-and-effect idea can be organized in four basic ways:

1. There can be one cause with one effect.

> EXAMPLE: Because the policeman saw me driving 40 mph on a 35 mph
> *cause*
>
> street, he gave me a ticket.
> *effect*

Can you think of an example showing one cause with one effect?

2. There can be many causes with one effect.

> EXAMPLE: The firefighter stated that poor electrical wiring, the severe thun-
> *cause* *cause*
>
> derstorm, and the burning candles caused the house to burn
> *cause* *cause*
>
> down.

Can you think of an example showing many causes with one effect?

3. There can be one cause leading to many effects.

> EXAMPLE: Because Sharon did not take her final U.S. history exam, she
> *cause*
>
> failed the course, was unable to graduate, and was taken off the
> *effect* *effect* *effect*
>
> school honor roll.

Can you think of an example showing one cause with many effects?

4. There can be many causes leading to many effects.

> **EXAMPLE**: Because the patient had poor dental hygiene and poor eating
> *cause*   *cause*
>
> habits, he now suffers from several cavities and serious gum
> *effect*   *effect*
>
> disease.

Can you think of an example showing many causes leading to many effects?

EXERCISE 1: Creating Your Own Cause-and-Effect Sentences

Following are several topics. For each one, create a good cause-and-effect sentence. Remember that you can have one effect for each cause or you can have many effects for each cause.

EXAMPLE

Topic: Someone broke a hip.

Sentence: Because John slipped and fell hard on the icy sidewalk, he broke his hip.

Topics

1. Someone caught a bad cold.
2. Someone had a great vacation.
3. A person you know is an excellent reader.
4. You just saw an automobile accident.
5. There has been an increase in crime in your neighborhood.
6. The city government has just raised the taxes where you now live.
7. You had a fight with a close friend or relative.

IMPORTANT VOCABULARY

The following words and phrases are commonly used in a cause-and-effect paper.

If . . . ., then . . . .
Because
Since
Due to

EXAMPLE

If you don't have a high-school diploma, *then* you cannot apply for the new secretarial position at the company.

To cause
To be the cause of
To be the effect of
To be the result of
To be the reason for
To contribute to
To result from
To result in

EXAMPLE

His stubborn pride *caused* him to lose a valuable friend.

So, thus
Therefore
Consequently
As a consequence
For this reason
As a result

EXAMPLE

Right at the last minute she lost her plane ticket; *consequently*, she was unable to fly to Paris with her friends.

EXERCISE 2: Practicing Cause-and-Effect Vocabulary

Find a partner. Take turns making statements orally using the words and phrases in the preceding list. Practice until you each have a chance to make at least seven sentences. Ask your teacher or an English speaker if you don't understand how to use any of the vocabulary items.

IMPORTANT PUNCTUATION: The Comma and Semicolon in Certain Cause-and-Effect Sentence Patterns

Here are some punctuation rules to remember when using the cause-and-effect vocabulary words.

A. If . . ., (then) . . .

   Because

   Since

   Due to

These expressions are used in subordinate clauses (expressing lesser facts and ideas). When the subordinate clause is at the beginning of the sentence, it is separated from the main clause (expressing principle ideas) by a comma. When the subordinate clause is at the end of the sentence, there is no comma separating it from the main clause.

EXAMPLE

If he doesn't come home by eight o'clock, John will miss the movie.

John will miss the movie *if* he doesn't come home by eight o'clock.

Due to the extremely icy conditions the sudden freeze had created, the road was closed.

The road was closed *due to* the extremely icy conditions the sudden freeze had created.

B. *So* separates two coordinating clauses (expressing equally important but dependent thoughts) in this manner:

   . . . . , so . . . .

EXAMPLES

Kevin has a test tomorrow, *so* he has to study tonight.

Ms. Taylor just got a big raise, *so* she is going to celebrate this weekend.

C. Thus

   Therefore

Consequently

As a consequence

For this reason

As a result

These expressions combine two independent clauses in this manner:

. . . .; therefore, ...

. . . .(.) Therefore, ...

EXAMPLES

Bob gained twenty pounds this winter; *as a result,* he is going on a diet this month.

Bob gained twenty pounds this winter. *As a result,* he is going on a diet this month.

Sarah broke her leg yesterday; *for this reason,* she won't be able to go on the bicycle trip tomorrow.

Sarah broke her leg yesterday. *For this reason,* she won't be able to go on the bicycle trip tomorrow.

EXERCISE 3: Practice Using Correct Punctuation with Cause-and-Effect Vocabulary

---

Pick seven of the words and phrases found in "Important Vocabulary" and write seven good cause-and-effect sentences with correct punctuation, spelling, and grammar. Show them to your instructor when you finish.

EXAMPLES

(*As a result*) The young boy accidently put his hand on the burning log; as a result, he burned himself badly.

(*If . . ., then . . .*) If you forget to water your plants for two months, they will probably die.

1. _____

2. _____

3. _____

4. _____

5. _____

6. _____

7. _____

GUIDED WRITING ACTIVITY

Think of a situation at your school that you consider to be a problem. You might, for example, be concerned with overcrowded classrooms, not having a student lounge, poor student government representation for foreign students, not having an athletics program, and so on. In this writing activity, you are going to present what you believe are the causes and effect of this problem at your school.

Peer Interaction

A. Get into groups of three or four.

B. STRATEGY FOR GATHERING INFORMATION

As a group, for about ten to fifteen minutes, you are going to make a list of all the different problems you can think of in your school (see page xiii for listmaking). Let your imagination go. Try to think of as many situations as you can.

C. Now take a few minutes to look at your group's list. Decide which problem most interests your group.

D. ANOTHER STRATEGY FOR GATHERING INFORMATION

Once you decide which problem you want to write about, you need to gather some information about the causes and the effect of this problem at your school. In order to develop information for causes and effects of your problem, you are first going to role play on paper (see page xiv for roleplaying). In other words you are going to write a rough, imaginary conversation between yourself and the person in your school who is best able to bring about a solution to the problem (this might be a teacher, student, president, program director, or counselor, for example). Follow these directions:

1. Take a piece of paper. For five minutes be yourself presenting to the other person what you feel are the causes and effect of this specific problem. Explain each point clearly.

2. Reread your comments. Now for five minutes respond to your comments

as the person who is best able to bring about a solution. Make comments and ask questions as if you were this other person. Let your imagination go.

3. Continue steps 1 and 2 until you feel that you have gathered enough information for your composition. The important thing to remember is that in step 1 you are writing as yourself. In step 2 you are writing as the person who can help you understand the problem.

4. When you finish the "conversation on paper," reread it carefully. Start to choose which information you want to use in your essay and which you don't.

E. Take a few minutes to share your problem and its causes and effect with the others in your group. Evaluate each other's information. Does it seem complete and interesting? Can you think of any other information to add? Help each other create strong explanations of the causes and effect of each problem. Also ask your teacher for help if you'd like.

F. Now try to decide the purpose of your paper. What point are you trying to make by explaining the causes and effect of your problem? Are you trying to show, for example, that it is possible to get rid of the causes and thus solve the problem? What point are you trying to make? Write it here:

_____

_____

G. Discuss each other's purposes. Do they seem logical and worth mentioning? Is each writer's purpose easy to understand? Is there anything he or she could do to improve the purpose?

H. Do you feel you are ready to begin working on a draft of your cause-and-effect paper? If not, review steps A through G until you feel you can begin writing.

Organizing Your Information

1. Now think about the information you have gathered on your problem, its causes, and its effect.

2. Try to organize this information into a clear, concise essay. Read the entire outline given here before you begin.

3. This outline is a suggestion to get you started. If you would like to modify it to suit your needs, better discuss your idea with your instructor and then go ahead.

Paragraph One: Introduction to the Problem

Briefly introduce the problem. Identify the causes of this problem. Mention the effects of this problem on you and on others in your school. Don't give a lot of detail. In the introduction, you just want to present the main idea to your readers.

What important information should be in the introduction? Write it here:

_____

_____

What is your thesis statement? Write it here:

_____

_____

Are you going to use any cause-and-effect vocabulary in this paragraph? Note them here:

_____

_____

Paragraph Two: The Causes of the Problem

What is your topic sentence for this paragraph? Write it here:

_____

_____

First Cause* Explain it here:

_____

_____

Second Cause* Explain it here:

_____

_____

*If your explanation of each cause is quite detailed, you may want to present each one in separate paragraphs.

Third Cause* Explain it here:

_____

_____

Are you going to use any cause-and-effect vocabulary in this paragraph? Note them here:

_____

_____

Paragraph Three: The Effect of the Problem

What is your topic sentence for this paragraph? Write it here:

_____

_____

The Effect. Explain it here:

_____

_____

Are you going to use any cause-and-effect vocabulary in this paragraph? Note them here:

_____

_____

Paragraph Four: The Conclusion

In your conclusion, bring the information from your introduction and body paragraphs together. In addition, try to add an interesting point. You might, for example, want to give a possible solution. You might want to give a prediction about what will happen if the problem is not solved. You might want to predict what the benefits will be if the problem is resolved. What interesting point would you like to add?

What is your topic sentence? Write it here:

_____

_____

What important information should be in your conclusion? Write it here:

_____

_____

Are you going to use any cause-and-effect vocabulary in this paragraph? Note them here:

_____

_____

What interesting point are you going to add? Write it here:

_____

_____

Rough Draft

Now using your notes, write the first draft of your composition.

Peer Editing

Find a partner and exchange your compositions. Follow these steps:

1. Read your partner's composition. Do not make any marks on the paper the first time you read it. Just try to get the main point.

2. Reread the paper. Underline any words, phrases, or expressions that don't seem correct or that are difficult to understand.

3. Do you have any questions about the contents of the composition? If so, write them on the Comments Sheet.

4. Now write three suggestions to the writer for improving his or her composition.

5. Give the composition and Comments Sheet to your partner.

Writing Your Final Draft

First consider the points from your partner's Comments Sheet. Put them into your rough draft if necessary. Then write the final draft of your composition.

Questions to Ask Yourself before Handing in Your Paper

Put a check mark in each box after you complete the tasks.

☐ Do I have a clear introduction with a good thesis statement?

☐ Do the paragraphs clearly present the points I am trying to make?

☐ Does each paragraph have enough information so that the reader can understand what I am saying?

☐ Have I used cause-and-effect vocabulary to help one idea flow smoothly into the next?

☐ Did I use the correct verb tense in each sentence? Are the words spelled correctly? Are my sentences structured well? Did I punctuate my sentences correctly?

When you finish your composition, give it to your instructor. After your instructor evaluates your composition, discuss it with him or her.

ADDITIONAL CAUSE-AND-EFFECT TOPICS

1. Find an animal that is on the endangered-species list and do some reading about it. Your teacher or librarian can help you get started. Write a paper in which you discuss the probable causes of this animal's near-extinction and its effect upon society.

2. Do some reading on the phenomenon of acid rain. Your teacher or a librarian can help you get started. Write a paper in which you discuss the probable cause of acid rain and its effects upon our society.

3. Discuss the effects on a society when its youth are poorly educated. You might want to look at effects directly related to the young people, short-term effects to society, and long-term effects to society.

4. Think of one success in your life. Discuss the probable causes of why it happened. Also discuss one effect it had on you.

5. Follow one major news story for a week by listening to the television and radio and reading the newspaper and news magazines. Then write a paper in which you discuss the probable effects this event will have on you personally.

6. Think of one music performer (or group) who is extremely popular today. Write a paper in which you discuss the probable causes of the performer's (or group's) popularity. Also examine one effect this popularity has on our society.

7. Think of a close friendship you had with someone that has now broken off or faded away. Discuss the probable causes of this broken or lost friendship and the effect it has had on you.

8

Comparison and Contrast

Sometimes when you write a paper, you want to discuss how two items are similar or how they are different. When you point out their similarities, we say that you are *comparing* the two items.* When you point out their differences, we say that you are *contrasting* the two items. Comparison and contrast is one of the most common writing patterns. You already use it every day informally when you decide such things as whether to wear long pants or shorts to the park. You will also use it quite often when writing formal papers at work or in school. Your sociology instructor might, for example, ask you to compare and contrast the types of jobs U.S. women held in the 1880s with those they hold in the 1980s. Your supervisor at work might ask you to write a report comparing and contrasting the qualifications of two advertising companies wanting your business. Because comparison and contrast is so widely used in writing, it is important to be familiar with its organization and to feel comfortable using it.

ORGANIZING A COMPARISON-AND-CONTRAST ESSAY

When using this writing pattern, you may choose only to compare the items or only to contrast them. Generally speaking, however, a writer will point out both similarities and differences between the two items. Regardless of whether you compare or contrast the subjects, it is important to pay careful attention to the arrangement of the material in the essay.

There are two basic ways in which the information in a comparison-and-contrast essay is organized. One is the *point approach*; the other is the *block approach*. When using the point approach, the writer makes a point about topic A and then immediately compares or contrasts that point with topic B. The writer then makes another point about topic A and immediately compares or contrasts it with topic B. This pattern is followed until the writer compares and contrasts, one by one, all the points about topic A and topic B. When using the block approach, in contrast, the writer explains all the points about topic A and then explains all the points about topic B. In other words, the writer gives blocks of information about each item. Following is information about the Apple IIc and the Apple IIe computers. Notice how the information is arranged in each approach.

Point Approach

Point 1: The Apple IIc, with its handle and lightweight case, is easy to pick up and carry.

The Apple IIe does not have a handle and is heavier. It cannot be moved as easily.

*It is important to note that people will often use the word *comparison* to mean both similarities and differences. If on a test, for example, a teacher asks you to compare subject A and subject B, he or she is very likely asking you to discuss both their similarities and differences.

Point 2: It is difficult to expand the hardware on the Apple IIc.

The Apple IIe can easily expand to use a variety of hardware.

Point 3: Apple IIc has 128K (information storage capability).

Apple IIe has only 64K (information storage capability).

Point 4: Apple IIc has a large selection of business, education, and entertainment computer programs.

Apple IIe also has a large selection of these types of programs.

Block Approach

Apple IIc: The Apple IIc, with its handle and lightweight case, is easy to pick up and carry.

It is difficult to expand the hardware on the Apple IIc.

The Apple IIc has 128K (information storage capability).

The Apple IIc has a large selection of business, education, and entertainment computer programs.

Apple IIe: The Apple IIe does not have a handle and is heavier than the Apple IIc. It cannot be moved as easily.

The Apple IIe can easily expand to use a variety of hardware.

The Apple IIe has 64K (information storage capability).

The Apple IIe has a large selection of business, education, and entertainment computer programs.

Comparison-and-Contrast Topics

Which topics should be compared and contrasted with each other? Can a person compare and contrast any two items? No. Compare and contrast topics only that come from the same general category or have some common characteristics. To compare two objects that have nothing in common is silly and a waste of time. There could be value in comparing the writing techniques of two mystery novelists, for instance, but why bother to compare a mystery writer's novels to a car mechanic's tools? Remember that as with other writing strategies, when comparing and contrasting two topics you have a purpose for doing so. You may, for example, be trying to make the point that A is better than B. Or, you may be trying to show that despite their obvious differences A and B are really very similar. Regardless of what point you are trying to make, you will soon find that it is almost impossible to do so if your two topics do not first have some common characteristics.

EXERCISE 1: Practice Organizing Comparison-and-Contrast Topics into Block and Point Patterns

Following are several comparison-and-contrast topics. As a class, think of several points you could make about each category. Write these points on the chalkboard. Divide the class into two groups. One group will organize the information into the point pattern. The other group will organize the same material into the block pattern. You don't have to use all the information on the board. Simply decide which points you want to use and which you don't. Try to think of a good thesis statement for the information and then organize it following the example here.

When you finish, put the point and block patterns on the chalkboard and evaluate them. Do they present the information accurately? Continue the exercise until all the topics have been put on the board. Each group should have a chance to practice both the block and point patterns.

EXAMPLE

The advantages of using a car or a motorcycle as a means of transportation

Student Responses: A motorcycle is less expensive.

A car offers more protection for motorists.

A motorcycle gets better gas mileage.

A car can comfortably take at least two people, usually more.

It is easier to find a parking space for a motorcycle than for a car.

A motorcycle is easier to have stolen.

A car is more comfortable against the weather.

Motorcycles help one enjoy the scenery more.

Block Approach

THESIS STATEMENT: For a student, it is wiser to purchase a motorcycle than a car although it does have some disadvantages.

Motorcycle

A motorcycle is less expensive than a car.

It gets better gas mileage than a car does.

Because it is so small, it is easy to find a parking space for it.

In a motorcycle, because you have no windows to inhibit the view, you can enjoy the scenery around you a lot more.

Car

The enclosed car offers more protection to the passengers from other cars and trucks.

A car can hold two or more people comfortably while a motorcycle can hold a maximum of two people.

Cars, because of their seats and trunk capacity, are able to carry many more goods such as groceries, laundry, and packages.

Point Approach

THESIS STATEMENT: Despite the cost of its purchase and maintenance, a car is a better buy than a motorcycle if you're looking for protection and comfort.

Cost

The purchase of a car is generally more expensive than the purchase of a motorcycle made in the same year.

Gas Mileage

The motorcycle gets much better gasoline mileage than does a car.

Parking

Because of its size, a motorcycle can often be parked in small, unconventional places. A car, however, needs a fairly standard parking space, which is larger than one needed for a motorcycle.

Passenger Protection

Because of their heavy metal frames and closed doors, cars, however, provide more physical safety to passengers during accidents than do motorcycles.

Vehicle Protection

Cars are enclosed and can be locked to keep people from getting inside them. Motorcycles are not enclosed vehicles. For this reason, cars are safer from theft than are motorcycles.

Passenger Comfort

It is true that motorcycles give an unrestricted view of the scenery around them; however, cars offer much more protection and comfort against bad weather such as extreme cold, heat, rain, snow, and strong winds.

Topics

1. Getting news by reading a newspaper or by watching television

2. Learning English as a second language in a classroom or learning it living with an American family

3. Looking for a job with a high-school diploma or looking for one with a bachelor's degree

4. The effects on your education when

   a. you live at home and go to school

   b. you live on the school campus and go to school

5. Having medical costs paid by the government or having medical costs paid by the individual

6. Working as a group to complete an assignment or working alone to complete an assignment

7. A vacation by the ocean or a vacation by a lake

EXERCISE 2: Finding Topics to Compare and Contrast

Comparing and contrasting is one of the writing patterns we use most often. Everywhere you look, subjects come to your attention that might make interesting topics for a comparison-and-contrast essay. For the next few days, pay close attention to what is going on around you. Make a list of topics about which you might want to create a comparison-and-contrast essay. Also think of the purpose or point you would make in comparing and contrasting each topic. Avoid obvious or very general topics like comparing your brother to your sister or comparing your old apartment to your new apartment. Really take some time to try to find unique topics that one might not notice quickly.

EXAMPLE

Topic: The evening programming on the public television channel and the evening programming on a national network

Purpose: To compare and contrast the type of audience (viewers) each channel hopes to attract

1. **Topic:** _____

   _____

   _____

   Purpose: _____

   _____

   _____

2. **Topic:** _____

   _____

   _____

   Purpose: _____

   _____

   _____

3. **Topic:** _____

   _____

   _____

   Purpose: _____

   _____

   _____

4. **Topic:** _____

   _____

   _____

   Purpose: _____

   _____

   _____

5. **Topic:** _____

   _____

   _____

   Purpose: _____

_____

_____

Which of these topics most interests you? Why? You might want to ask your instructor if you could substitute this topic for the guided writing activity at the end of this chapter.

IMPORTANT VOCABULARY

The following words and phrases are often used in a comparison-and-contrast essay. Pay special attention to the punctuation used in the examples.

To Show Comparison

To resemble
To be the same as
To be similar to
To be like
To be equal to
Comparable to
To be as _____ as

Walkers *resemble* joggers; both seek to exercise their hearts and lungs.

Walkers *are comparable to* joggers; both seek to exercise their hearts and lungs.

Walkers *are as concerned as* joggers about improving their physical fitness.

Both _____ and _____
Neither _____ nor _____
Not only _____ but also

Both police officers *and* lawyers must be very familiar with the city's laws.

Neither police officers *nor* lawyers can afford not to know the city's laws well.

Not only police officers *but also* lawyers must be very familiar with the city's laws.

Similarly
In the same way
Likewise
Correspondingly

Registration for day classes begins on May 19; *similarly,* registration for night classes begins at 4:00 P.M. that same day.

Registration for day classes begins on May 19. *Likewise,* registration for night classes begins at 4:00 P.M. that same day.

Like	*Like* the TOEFL test, the MTELP measures a student's ESL skills.
	Like soccer, basketball divides its games into quarters.

To Show Contrast

-er _____ than	New York City is *bigger than* St. Louis.
More _____ than	New York City is *more crowded than* St. Louis.
Less _____ than	St. Louis is *less crowded than* New York City.
Not as _____ as	St. Louis is *not as big as* New York City.

Contrasts with	Ice cream *differs from* ice milk in that ice cream contains more fat.
Differs from	Ice cream *is different from* ice milk. Ice cream contains more fat.
Is different from	

Although	*Although* you can drive 45 mph on State Line Road, you can drive only 30 mph on Mission Road.
Whereas	You can drive only 30 mph on Mission Road *although* you can drive 45 mph on State Line Road.
While	

However	My sister likes to go to scary movies; *however*, I hate to watch them.
On the other hand	My sister likes to go to scary movies. *On the other hand*, I hate to watch them.
On the contrary	
In contrast	

Unlike	*Unlike* the typewriter, the word processor allows a person to insert and delete information while typing.
Contrary to	*In contrast to* the typewriter, the word processor allows a person to insert and delete information while typing.
In contrast to	
In opposition to	

EXERCISE 3: Practice Making Comparison-and-Contrast Sentences

Find a partner. Choose a word or phrase from the preceding lists. Your partner will identify the word or phrase as either an expression of comparison or an expression of contrast. He or she will then make a good statement using that word. Repeat until you both have a chance to make several sentences. Ask your teacher or an English speaker if you do not understand how to use any of the vocabulary items.

EXERCISE 4: More Practice Making Comparison-and-Contrast Sentences

Following is a list of general topics. For each one, make a comparison and a contrast using the vocabulary from the lists.

EXAMPLE: (two cars you've driven)

Comparison: My 1970 Volkswagen is the same as my 1982 Subaru in that they both have stick shifts.

Contrast: My 1982 Subaru has a heater and carpeting; on the other hand, my 1970 Volkswagen has neither.

1. (two classmates)

   Comparison: _____

   _____

   Contrast: _____

   _____

2. (two types of American food)

   Comparison: _____

   _____

   Contrast: _____

   _____

3. (two English books you are using)

   Comparison: _____

   _____

Contrast: _____

_____

4. (two movies you've recently seen)

Comparison: _____

_____

Contrast: _____

_____

5. (two sports or games you play)

Comparison: _____

_____

Contrast: _____

_____

IMPORTANT PUNCTUATION/USAGE:
Sentence Combining

Often when writing a comparison-and-contrast essay you want to combine two ideas into one sentence. Sometimes you want to compare two ideas; other times you want to contrast them. The punctuation for these sentences differs depending on the expressions you use. Let's review some of the more difficult rules.

A. Subordinate Adverbial Clauses

Although

Whereas

While

EXAMPLES

Although he wanted to visit Chicago, Peter went with his family to San Francisco.

Peter went with his family to San Francisco *although* he wanted to visit Chicago.

Whereas Sam went to the University of Colorado to study, his best friend went to the University of Texas.

His best friend went to the University of Texas *whereas* Sam went to the University of Colorado.

If you have questions about this sentence pattern, review "Important Punctuation," section A of chapter seven.

B. Linking Two Independent Clauses

Comparison	Contrast
Similarly	However
In the same way	On the other hand
Likewise	On the contrary
Correspondingly	In contrast

EXAMPLES

Laurie is going to learn to speak Spanish; *likewise,* Robert is going to learn to speak Arabic.

Laurie is going to learn to speak Spanish. *Likewise,* Robert is going to learn to speak Arabic.

Joan decided to quit her job when she didn't get a raise; *in contrast,* Virginia decided to keep hers.

Joan decided to quit her job when she didn't get a raise. *In contrast,* Virginia decided to keep hers.

If you have questions about this sentence pattern, review "Important Punctuation," section C of chapter seven.

C. Prepositional Phrases

Comparison	Contrast
Like	Unlike
	Contrary to
	In contrast to
	In opposition to

The prepositional phrase has a preposition followed by a noun or pronoun. These prepositional phrases can be found at the beginning of a sentence or inserted in the middle of it. When the prepositional phrase is at the beginning of a sentence, it is *not* separated from the main clause by a comma unless it is unusually long. When the prepositional phrase is inserted into the main clause of the sentence, however, it is separated by commas.

EXAMPLES

Unlike push-ups running exercises one's cardiovascular system.

Running, unlike push-ups, exercises one's cardiovascular system.

In contrast to today's soccer game yesterday's was dull and slow.

Yesterday's game, in contrast to today's soccer game, was dull and slow.

EXERCISE 5: Practice Combining Sentences

Following are groups of several short sentences. Combine each group into one sentence using the word or phrase in parentheses. Remember to use pronoun reference where applicable. If you have difficulty, review the "Important Vocabulary" and "Important Punctuation" sections in this chapter or ask your instructor for help.

Example

Chemistry I has a required laboratory period. Biology I also has a required laboratory period.

(*Both . . . and . . .*) Both Chemistry I and Biology I have a required laboratory period.

1. The plane could only land on an airport runway. The helicopter could land on a rocky field.

   (while) _____

   _____

2. I lost my credit card in the department store. Andy lost his credit card in the restaurant.

   (likewise) _____

   _____

3. Sally got better quickly because she went to the doctor. Ted stayed sick for several weeks because he didn't go to the doctor.

   (on the other hand) _____

   _____

4. Canned green beans contain a lot of salt. Fresh and frozen green beans don't have a lot of salt.

(more _____ than) _____

_____

5. The self-assured woman was convicted of kidnapping the baby. The frightened man was also found guilty of the crime.

   (to be like) _____

   _____

6. Elizabeth always studies for her exams. Ann never studies for her exams.

   (is different from) _____

   _____

7. At a stop sign one must come to a complete stop. At a yield sign one may slow down and then proceed with caution.

   (although) _____

   _____

8. Brownfield Industries produces only ballpoint pens. Carson Enterprises produces ballpoint pens, pencils, and felt-tipped markers.

   (unlike) _____

   _____

9. Jason went on a diet and didn't lose any weight. Lincoln went on a diet and didn't lose any weight either.

   (neither . . . nor . . .) _____

   _____

10. Kathryn is very outgoing. Lisa is very shy.

    (not as . . . as) _____

    _____

11. At the beginning of the semester John could only write one sentence in English. At the end of the semester John could write a whole paragraph in English.

    (in contrast) _____

    _____

12. The artist's last painting contains subtle shades of pink and gray. The artist's newest painting contains subtle shades of pink and gray.

(resemble) _____

_____

13. The author's latest book has been a best seller for ten weeks. The author's first book was a best seller for ten weeks.

(like) _____

_____

14. Professor Hawks is very serious in class. Professor Banks is very humorous in class.

(differs from) _____

_____

15. Joe eats a lot when he gets nervous. Jack doesn't eat anything when he gets nervous.

(contrary to) _____

_____

EXERCISE 6: Practice Using Correct Punctuation with Comparison-and-Contrast Vocabulary

In this exercise you are going to practice creating your own comparison-and-contrast sentences. First, look at the topic that follows. Take a few minutes to make some notes about it in the space provided.

TOPIC: Learning English in your own country and learning English in North America

Notes for Learning English in Your Own Country

Notes for Learning English in North America

Now make up comparison-and-contrast sentences using the information you have noted. In every sentence, use one of the following expressions:

Similarly

Neither . . . nor . . .

To be similar to

Likewise

Like

Differs from

Although

However

Unlike

While

GUIDED WRITING ACTIVITY

Busy streets in a city have a different feeling or "personality" in the day than they do at night. For example, you may notice different types of people in the daytime than those you notice at night. The types of activities going on are different in the morning and at night. Even the physical appearance of the street is quite different. In this writing activity, you are going to compare and contrast some of these differences based on your own observations.

Peer Interaction

A. As a class decide which street in your city you would like to observe.* In order to gather enough information for your essay, it is important to choose a street that is quite busy both in the daytime and at night. Of course, no place is completely safe, but try to pick a street that is found in a generally safe area.

B. Pick some time both during the day and night when you can visit the street and observe what is going on. It might be a good idea to go as a class or at least in groups. It will make the experience more fun; in addition, you can share observations with each other.**

---

*If you prefer you can choose individually or in small groups which street you would like to visit.
**You can gather your details from memory if it is not possible to visit the street; however, observing the street in person is strongly encouraged.

C. STRATEGY FOR GATHERING INFORMATION

While you are visiting the street, make some rough notes of what you observe (see pages xiii–xiv for observing). Have one piece of paper for your day observations and one for your night observations. Write down both *objective* and *subjective* details. (See page 36 if you need to review objective and subjective details.) Don't worry about grammar or spelling. Just collect as much information as you can.

D. As soon as you can, try to organize your details on each piece of paper under the topics of types of people, types of activities, and physical appearance of the street. Choose other categories for your details if you prefer.

The Street in the Daytime	*The Street at Night*
Types of People	Types of People
Types of Activities	Types of Activities
Physical Appearance of the Street	Physical Appearance of the Street

E. Get into groups of three or four. Compare the notes you have taken about the street. Combine your ideas under each category either on the board or on a piece of paper.

F. Right now you probably have quite a bit of information under each category, but are there any ideas you can add? With your group discuss the information and add to the lists any information you think of.

G. Now look at the information you have gathered. You will probably not want to use all of it. Can you begin to see which pieces of information you want to use and which you don't? Ask your teacher for help if you'd like.

H. Try to decide on the purpose of this essay. What point are you trying to make by comparing and contrasting the feeling of this street during the day and at night? Are you trying to show that this street is a place of work during the day but a place to play at night? Once you decide on the purpose of your essay, write it here.

Purpose: _____

_____

I. Discuss each other's purposes. Do they seem logical and worth mentioning? Is each writer's purpose easy to understand? Is there anything he or she could do to improve it?

J. Think about how you are going to organize your information about this street in the day and at night. Are you going to use the point approach or the block approach? Very briefly organize the *main* ideas of your paper in one of the two patterns that follow:

POINT APPROACH

1. **Types of People**

   A. During the day_____

   _____

   B. At night_____

   _____

2. **Types of Activities**

   A. During the day_____

   _____

   B. At night_____

   _____

3. **Physical Appearance of the Street**

   A. During the day_____

   _____

   B. At night_____

   _____

BLOCK APPROACH

1. **The Street during the Day**

   A. Types of people_____

   _____

   B. Types of activities_____

   _____

C. Physical appearance of the street _____

_____

2. **The Street at Night**

   A. Types of people _____

_____

   B. Types of activities _____

_____

   C. Physical appearance of the street _____

_____

   K. Do you feel that you are ready to begin working on a draft of the essay? If not, review steps B through J (either alone or as a group) until you feel you are ready to begin.

Organizing Your Information

   1. Now think about the information you have gathered for these two street scenes. In what ways are they the same? In what ways are they different? Also think again about your purpose for writing this essay.

   2. Try to organize this information into a clear, concise essay. Read the entire outline given here before you begin.

   3. This outline is a suggestion to get you started. If you would like to modify it to suit your needs better, discuss your idea with your teacher and then go ahead.

Paragraph One: Introduction to the Street Scene

   Briefly introduce the idea that you are comparing and contrasting a busy street in your city based on personal observations. Let the reader know exactly which street it is. You might even want to explain briefly where the street is located. Also explain your purpose for comparing and contrasting this street in the daytime and at night. Don't give a lot of detail. In the introduction, you just want to present the main ideas to your reader.

What important information should be in your introduction? Write it here:

_____

_____

What is your thesis statement? Write it here:

_____

_____

Is there any comparison-and-contrast vocabulary that could be used here? Write out sentences using appropriate expressions.

_____

_____

Paragraph Two: Types of People on the Street during the Day and at Night*

What is your topic sentence for this paragraph? Write it here:

_____

_____

What important information are you going to mention about the two street scenes? Write it here:

_____

_____

What examples, facts, and details are you going to use to support your basic information in this paragraph? Explain them here:

_____

_____

Is there any comparison-and-contrast vocabulary that could be used here? Write out sentences using the appropriate expressions.

_____

_____

Paragraph Three: Types of Activities on the Street during the Day and at Night**

What is your topic sentence for this paragraph? Write it here:

*If you are going to use the block instead of the point approach, this paragraph will present all the ideas about the street scene during the day.
**If you are going to use the block instead of the point approach, this paragraph will present all the ideas about the street scene at night.

_____

_____

What important information are you going to mention about the two street scenes? Write it here:

_____

_____

What examples, facts, or details are you going to use to support your basic information in this paragraph? Explain them here:

_____

_____

Is there any comparison-and-contrast vocabulary that could be used here? Write out sentences using the appropriate expressions.

_____

_____

Paragraph Four: The Physical Appearance of the Street during the Day and at Night*

What is your topic sentence for this paragraph? Write it here:

_____

_____

What important information are you going to mention about the two street scenes? Write it here:

_____

_____

What examples, facts, and details are you going to use to support your basic information in this paragraph? Explain them here:

_____

_____

*If you are going to use the block instead of the point approach, you will not have this paragraph.

Is there any comparison-and-contrast vocabulary that could be used here? Write out sentences using the appropriate expressions.

Last Paragraph: The Conclusion

    In your conclusion, bring together the information from your introduction and body paragraphs; in addition, try to add an interesting point. You might want to mention an amusing incident you saw during the day or at night which is significant to your essay. You might want to mention something interesting you learned about this street by observing it both during the day and at night. What interesting point would you like to add?

What is your topic sentence? Write it here:

What important information should be in your conclusion? Write it here:

What interesting point are you going to add? Write it here:

Is there any comparison-and-contrast vocabulary that could be used here? Write out sentences using appropriate expressions.

Rough Draft

    Now using your notes, write the first draft of your composition.

Peer Editing

    Find a partner and exchange your compositions. Follow these steps:

1. Read your partner's composition. Do not make any marks on the paper the first time you read it. Just try to get the main point.

2. Reread the paper. Underline any words, phrases, or expressions that don't seem correct or that are difficult to understand.

3. Do you have any questions about the contents of the composition? If so, write them on the Comments Sheet.

4. Now write three suggestions to the writer for improving his or her composition.

5. Give the composition and Comments Sheet to your partner.

Writing Your Final Draft

First consider the points from your partner's Comments Sheet. Add them to your rough draft if needed. Then write the final draft of your composition.

Questions to Ask Yourself before Handing in Your Paper

Put a check mark in each box after you complete the tasks.

☐ Do I have a clear introduction with a good thesis statement?

☐ Do the paragraphs clearly present the points I am trying to make?

☐ Does each paragraph have enough information so that the reader can understand what I am saying?

☐ Have I used comparison-and-contrast vocabulary?

☐ Did I remember to use sentences that have subordinate adverbial clauses, two independent clauses, and prepositional phrases similar to the sample sentences presented in this chapter?

When you finish your composition, give it to your instructor. After your instructor evaluates your composition, discuss it with him or her.

ADDITIONAL COMPARISON-AND-CONTRAST TOPICS

1. Compare and contrast the lifestyle of a person who sleeps nights and works days with a person who sleeps days and works nights.

2. Compare and contrast the advantages and disadvantages of running for exercise and walking for exercise.

3. Compare and contrast a social custom in your country and in North America. Some suggestions:

dating

New Year's celebration

funeral

birthday

4. Compare and contrast the care of the elderly in your country and in North America. You will probably first need to get some information about the care of the elderly in North America by reading, talking with Americans, and so on.

5. Compare and contrast two similar businesses in North America: one that you liked and one that you didn't. Some suggestions:

two banks

two department stores

two supermarkets

two fastfood restaurants

6. Compare and contrast two local or national news reporters in North America. Consider their presentation of the news, their credibility, and their likability.

7. Compare and contrast two different types of computers with which you are familiar.

9

Definition

Sometimes when you are writing a paper you want to explain to your reader what an unknown term or phrase means. This is called *definition*. If you want to describe briefly an unfamiliar term within an essay, this is called *a short definition*. If the primary purpose of your paper is to explain fully the meaning of the word, this is called *an extended definition*.

THE SHORT DEFINITION

In the short definition you do the following three things:

1. State the word

2. Tell what class or group the word belongs to

3. Tell what makes this word different from all the others in this particular class or group.

Look at the following examples. Can you identify the different parts of each sentence that make it a good short definition?

> The *human heart* is a *muscular organ of the body* that *maintains the circulation of the blood by acting as a pump.*
>
> A *sled* is a *type of vehicle* that *has two runners and is used for transportation on snow and ice.*
>
> An *orthodontist* is *a dentist* who *deals specifically with correcting teeth that aren't aligned properly.*

We often use the short definition to explain a highly technical or specialized term that would generally not be known to the reader. When defining a term, it is important not to repeat some form of the word in the definition itself because it doesn't really tell the reader any new information. Look at the following two examples of weak definitions:

> A mathematician is a person who works in the field of mathematics.
>
> A drive-in theater is a theater where you drive your car in to watch the movie.

Can you change these two definitions so that they are stronger?

THE EXTENDED DEFINITION

The extended definition is different from the short definition in that it is not just one or two sentences of an essay. Rather, it is the whole essay itself.

We often use the extended definition to explain the meaning of words that are well known but abstract (not specific or factual). Some examples of abstract words are *love, honesty, freedom,* and *respect.* Obviously, words like these are going to have many different meanings or interpretations. Your job in an extended definition, then, is to explain what you think a term means in a certain situation or purpose. For example, the way you define *honesty* in terms of the business world might be very different from the way you define it in terms of being true to oneself.

There are several different ways we extend a definition into a complete essay. We have already learned many of these ways in earlier chapters. We can extend a definition by one or a combination of several of the following:

1. Explaining the term by giving several examples or one long example. (See the chapter on illustration.)

2. Explaining the term by describing it. (See the chapter on description.)

3. Explaining the term by classifying it into different categories and then explaining each category. (See the chapter on classification.)

4. Explaining the term by giving a brief chronological history of the development of the word. (See the section on chronological order in the chapter on narration.)

Another way to define a word is by stating what it is not followed by stating what it is. Here is an example of this type of extended definition.

Just What Is a Vacation Anyway?

A vacation is generally seen as a very positive experience. In fact, when a person says, "I'm on vacation" or "I'm leaving for my vacation," we all smile and offer our congratulations to the lucky guy. It's as if we collectively agree upon what this man is about to experience. It is my contention, however, that we do not agree upon what makes up a vacation. In fact, I believe that most of us don't even understand what a vacation truly is.

Many people seem to think that a vacation is merely a two-week reprieve from their place of employment. Well, a vacation cannot be defined in terms of "two weeks off." First of all, some people get a four-week vacation while others get only one. Some people get no days off from work but still manage to take a very nice vacation from time to time. What about the people who don't "go to work" such as mothers at home? Their idea of a vacation may be a weekend break from their children. The break may be a short time, but this makes it no less of a vacation for the person taking it.

Other people consider a vacation to be a period of rest. While a vacation is often a time of relaxation and quiet thoughts, it certainly doesn't have to be so. How many times have you gone back to work or school from a vacation more exhausted than when you left? For many people, taking a vacation means action — swimming, hiking, boating, running, driving. If they are not moving, then it really isn't a vacation to them.

Still others think it isn't a vacation unless they have gone away somewhere. To support this, invariably the first question we ask someone after her vacation is, "Oh, where did you go on your vacation?" My parents fall into this category of vacationers. Not only do they tend to go somewhere on their vacation, but they often plan up to a year in advance where they'll be going next. Not all people like to "get away," though. Many like to stay home during their holiday, yet they have no less of a vacation than my wandering parents.

The last group of vacationers feel that the vacation is a time to catch up on all the things they normally don't have time to do. This, to me, seems like work, but to others it is truly a vacation. These are the people who will tell you, "I had the most wonderful vacation. I got the house painted, cleaned out the garage, and fixed the broken fan and vacuum cleaner!" I know that this cannot be the true definition of a vacation because I take a vacation every year, and I would *never* paint my house during one.

Well, then, just what is a vacation? A vacation is a time to leave (to vacate). In other words, it is an indeterminate amount of time in which a person departs from his or her ordinary routine to do something out of the ordinary. So, a vacation is not a two-week break from the office, a ride down a river, or a trip to a new city although any of these things could be included in one. Vacations are simply a chance to change for a while. That is why, regardless of their form, we like them so much.

Discussion Questions

1. What is this essay defining?

2. What is the thesis, or purpose, of this essay?

3. How did the writer organize each body paragraph? In other words, how did the writer present the information?

4. Did the author state what vacations are not in his or her opinion? Specifically what were these incorrect definitions of vacation?

5. Where was the correct definition of vacation, according to the writer, found in this essay?

6. Do you agree with this definition of vacation? Why? Why not?

7. Do you now understand how to organize a definition paper in which one states what the term is not? If not, ask your instructor for help.

EXERCISE 1: Practice Writing Good Short Definitions

For each of the words that follow try to write a good short definition. If you are unfamiliar with a word, ask your instructor to explain it to you or look it up in a dictionary. Remember, a short definition should (1) state the term, (2) state which group the term belongs to, and (3) explain what makes this word different from all the others in this group. Share your definitions with the others in your class.

EXAMPLE: typewriter

A typewriter is a machine that prints letters on paper by metal keys striking through an inked ribbon.

1. motorcycle

2. poem

3. biology

4. a watch

5. anesthesiologist

6. thermometer

7. honeymoon

8. theorem

9. toaster

10. financier

EXERCISE 2: Practice Finding Ways to Develop an Extended Definition

---

Remember that there are a variety of ways to extend a definition. In this exercise you are going to practice thinking of different ways to extend a definition for each of the abstract terms that follow. If you can think of more than one way to extend a particular term, make note of each of them. Share your answers with each other. Notice the many different ways it is possible to extend a word.

EXAMPLE: Honesty

Short Definition: Honesty is a form of behavior in which a person is fair, straightforward, and sincere with the people with whom he or she deals.

Extended by: Examples

1. A person who returned a lost wallet with money
2. A person who confronted a friend about his drug problem even though all his other friends ignored it
3. A person who didn't lie about problems at work even though it would probably cost him his job

1. freedom

   Short Definition: _____

   _____

   Extended by:

2. respect

   Short Definition: _____

   _____

   Extended by:

3. anxiety

   Short Definition: _____

   _____

   Extended by:

4. greed

   Short Definition: _____

   _____

   Extended by:

5. competition

Short Definition: _____

_____

Extended by:

IMPORTANT VOCABULARY

The following words and phrases are commonly used in a definition paper:

Is
Means
Signifies
Refers to
Constitutes
Is considered to be

EXAMPLES

The extended definition *refers to* a lengthy explanation of a word in which a term is fully explained through the use of such techniques as examples, classification, or description.

In slang the term "jam" *constitutes* a state of being in which a person finds himself or herself in a difficult situation.

It was stated earlier, remember, that often in the extended definition we are giving our own interpretation of a term. In these cases, some expressions can be added to the vocabulary words in the preceding list:

To me (the term)	is
What I mean by (the term) is that it	means
In this context (the term)	signifies
In this situation (the term)	refers to
For this purpose (the term)	consitutes
	is considered to be

EXAMPLES

Let's look at parenthood. *In this context* love *means* taking care of all the needs of one's child.

To me security *constitutes* a good home, warm clothing, and enough food to eat.

EXERCISE 3: Practicing Definition Vocabulary

Find a partner. Think of a word or phrase to be defined. Your partner will choose an expression from the definition vocabulary lists and make a good definition. Repeat until you both have a chance to make several definitions. Try to choose a mixture of technical and abstract terms. (It might be fun to select some of the new words you have been learning in your English class.) Ask your teacher for help if you don't understand how to use any of the vocabulary items.

EXERCISE 4: More Definition Vocabulary Practice

Following is a list of several words. Choose one from the list or choose one of your own and then write a good sentence using the expression in parentheses. Ask your teacher for help if you don't understand how to use any of the vocabulary items.

TERMS: failure, videocassette recorder, ignorance, prejudice, exams, a friend, maturity, heart attack, war, peace, a brother or sister, catastrophe, credit card, a movie star, envy.

1. (means) _____

_____

2. (to me) _____

_____

3. (in this context) _____

_____

4. (is considered to be) _____

_____

5. (constitutes) _____

_____

6. (what I mean by [the term] is) _____

_____

7. (refers to) _____

_____

IMPORTANT PUNCTUATION/USAGE: The Complex Sentence and the Compound-Complex Sentence

In the chapter on illustration (chapter three) you learned about the simple sentence and the compound sentence. In this chapter, you are going to learn about two more sentence types: the complex sentence and the compound-complex sentence. Using all four of these sentence types in your essays can help add a great deal of variety to your writing.

The Complex Sentence

The complex sentence has two parts:

1. An independent clause
2. A dependent clause

The independent clause is a complete thought and can stand as a sentence by itself. The dependent clause, however, is not a complete thought. It needs to be attached to (or depend upon) the independent clause to get its meaning. Furthermore, the dependent clause is less important than the idea expressed in the independent clause. Look at the following examples:

Since Jack wrecked his car, he has had no way to get to work.

    dependent clause   *independent clause*

Mohammad is going to go back to his country after he finishes this semester.

    independent clause   *dependent clause*

Even though he desperately wanted to, the little boy didn't take the chocolate

    dependent clause   *independent*

candy bar.

    clause

As you can see, the dependent clause can come either before or after the independent clause in a complex sentence. If it comes before, it is generally separated from the independent clause by a comma. If it comes after, generally there is no comma between the independent and dependent clauses.

The dependent clause of a complex sentence always begins with a dependent word. Here are several of the most common dependent words. Ask your instructor if you don't understand any of them.

To Express Time

After, Before, Since, Until, When, While, As

While Sara was getting ready for bed, she heard someone fire a gun.
I have been living in this apartment *since* the day John moved out.

To Express Cause

Because, Since, As

Because Mark is only seventeen years old, he cannot vote yet.
Ted refused to buy the chair *since* it had a scratch on it.

To Express Condition

If, Unless

Unless the company sells more cars next year, it is going to go broke.

To Express Concession

Although, Even though, Though

Ben did not get accepted by the university *although* he had good grades and several recommendations.

To Express Purpose

In order to, So that

My father took an extra job *so that* our family could take a vacation this summer.

For an Expression of Identification

That, When, Where, Which, Who

I want to talk to the little girl *who* is wearing the plaid dress.
Elizabeth chose the dog *that* was running around and barking.

The Compound-Complex Sentence

The compound-complex sentence is made up of the following:

1. An independent clause (in the form of a compound sentence)
2. A dependent clause (like those mentioned above)

As in the complex sentence, the independent clause of the compound-complex sentence is a complete thought while the dependent clause is not. It must be attached to the independent clause (the compound sentence) to get its meaning and is considered to be less important than the independent clause. Look at the following examples:

<u>While the rock band was playing,</u> <u>a young girl fainted and a little boy screamed</u>

      dependent clause   *independent clause in the form of a*

<u>at the top of his lungs.</u>

  compound sentence

<u>The man ate shrimp and the woman sipped champagne</u> <u>while the waiter served</u>

     independent clause (compound sentence)   *dependent*

<u>them both dessert.</u>

   clause

Remember that the dependent clause can come either before or after the independent clause in a compound-complex sentence. If it comes before, it is generally separated from the independent clause by a comma. If it comes after, there is no comma between the independent and dependent clauses.

EXERCISE 5: Practice Making Complex Sentences

Combine the following simple sentences into good complex sentences. Use one of the dependent words listed in the preceding section to introduce your dependent clause. In most cases there will be more than one acceptable choice. Use pronoun reference when necessary. Be sure that your sentences make sense. Share your sentences with each other.

EXAMPLE

The secretary didn't come to work for three days.
The boss fired the secretary.

Because the secretary didn't come to work for three days, her boss fired
her.

I chose the used car.
The used car had an automatic transmission.

I chose the used car that had an automatic transmission.

1. You go to the dentist for an appointment.

   You brush your teeth.

   _____

   _____

2. Julie studied hard for the test.

   Julie did not pass the test.

   _____

   _____

3. You put money into a savings account.

   The money will earn interest every year.

   _____

   _____

4. I don't like to watch the newscaster on television. (who)

   The newscaster on television never smiles.

   _____

   _____

5. The pilot refused to fly the jet. (that)

   The jet hadn't been checked by the mechanics.

   _____

   _____

6. The doctor examined the patient in her office.

   The doctor sent the patient to the hospital for more tests.

   _____

   _____

7. You have the lucky number on your game card.

   You will win a nice prize.

   _____

   _____

8. I got out of the car.

   I realized I had locked my keys inside the car.

   _____

   _____

9. I'd like to go out to lunch with the new lady. (who)

   The new lady works in our office.

   _____

   _____

10. I'd like to buy the oven. (which)

    The oven cleans itself automatically.

    _____

    _____

11. Alex was reading a murder mystery.

    Sam was watching a murder mystery on the television.

    _____

    _____

12. The little girl pretended to be sick.

    The little girl could stay home from school.

    _____

    _____

EXERCISE 6: Practice Making Compound-Complex Sentences

In this exercise you are going to create your own compound-complex sentences using the words in parentheses. Really let your imagination go; write down interesting thoughts. Share your sentences with each other.

Example: (and, while)

While the robber was trying to hold up the gas station, a customer hit him on the head with a lead pipe and the manager called the police.

1. (but, after) _____

_____

2. (and, if) _____

_____

3. (so, because) _____

_____

4. (and, so that) _____

_____

5. (but, while) _____

_____

6. (and, although) _____

_____

7. (and, before) _____

_____

8. (but, since) _____

_____

9. (or, even though) _____

_____

10. (and, in order to) _____

_____

GUIDED WRITING ACTIVITY

One of the most interesting aspects of any language is its *slang expressions*. A slang expression can be defined as a word or phrase that is generally composed of nonstandard vocabulary and is used by a certain group of people such as teenagers or college students. Here are two current slang expressions used in North American English:

Yuppie: a young upwardly mobile professional

to chill out: to relax, to become calm or less hyperactive

Slang expressions are particularly interesting because they add color and variety to a language. They are sometimes difficult to understand, even for native speakers, because they come in and out of fashion so quickly and because the words' slang meaning is generally very different from their literal meaning. In this writing activity, you are going to have a chance to learn about and define one of the current slang expressions used in North American English.

Peer Interaction

A. Get into groups of three or four. Look at the slang expressions your teacher has listed. Together decide which expression your group would like to learn more about and then define it. (You can define a slang expression not found on the list if it interests you more.)

B. STRATEGY FOR GATHERING INFORMATION

In order to gather information for this assignment, you are going to need first to question several people. By yourself or in pairs, interview several native speakers about this slang expression (see page xiii for interviewing). Remember that when you talk to native speakers, your purpose is to find out what they think the word means and how it is used. To get you started, here is a list of questions you could ask them. Add any other questions you would like. Either during the interview or very soon after, write down what the people said so that you won't forget it.

Possible Interview Questions

(First introduce yourself; then explain what you are doing and why.)

1. Do you know what this expression means? (State the expression.) I just learned it and am not too sure what it means.

2. How do you use it? That is, in which situations is it appropriate to say this slang expression?

3. Which people generally use this slang expression? children? teenagers? college students? someone else?

4. Are there any situations where one should definitely not use this slang expression? What are they? Are there certain types of people around whom one should not use this expression?

5. How do you think this expression got started? How long has it been popular? Where did you first hear it?

6. Can you give me an example of an actual situation in which a person might use this expression?

7. Add any other question you would like to ask.

C. After you interview several people, get back in your groups to compare information. Discuss the answers to your interview questions. It might be a good idea to write down on a piece of paper all the examples of how the slang expression is used so that they are available to everyone. Does it seem that by putting your ideas together you have gathered enough information to help you define this slang term? Does it seem interesting and worth discussing? If not, you may need to interview a few more people. Also ask your teacher for help if you'd like.

D. Now think about how you plan to develop your definition of this slang term. It may be easiest to define it by using several examples, since you have already gathered this information during your interviews. You may, however, want to define the term by explaining what it is not or by giving a little history of its development in the language. Organize the information you have so far according to the way you plan to develop your definition of this slang expression. If you plan to use examples to explain his term, for example, roughly organize your information into the different examples you are going to use. If you are going to classify this term into categories, roughly organize your information into the different categories you are going to use.

E. Think of the purpose of this essay. Why are you using this information to define this slang expression? What point are you trying to make? Are you trying to make the point, for example, that this phrase's slang meaning is entirely different from its literal one? Are you trying to make the point that this slang expression has several different meanings depending upon who is using it? Are you trying to make some entirely different point? Write your purpose here:

_____

_____

F. Get together again with the others in your group. This time take a few minutes to discuss each other's purposes. Also discuss how each person plans to develop his or her definition. Does the writer's purpose seem logical and worth mentioning? Is it easy to understand? Does it seem to be supported by the writer's information? Is there anything you could do to improve the writer's purpose? Does it seem as if the purpose will be well supported by the way the writer is going to develop his or her definition (examples, comparison and contrast, and so on)?

G. Do you feel you are ready to begin working on a draft of your process paper? If not, review steps A through F until you feel you can begin writing.

Organizing Your Information

1. Now think about the information you have gathered to define this slang expression. Also think about the point you are trying to make by explaining this slang term.

2. Try to organize this information into a clear, concise essay. Read the entire outline given here before you begin.

3. This outline is a suggestion to get you started. If you would like to modify it to suit your needs better, discuss your idea with your teacher and then go ahead.

Paragraph One: The Introduction to Your Definition

In this paragraph, briefly introduce the idea that you are defining a slang expression currently used in North America. This would be a good place to write a strong short definition stating the slang expression, the group to which it belongs, and its distinguishing characteristics. Also briefly explain your purpose or reason for defining it. Don't give a lot of detail. In the introduction, you just want to present the main idea to your reader.

What important information should be in your introduction? Write it here:

_____

_____

What is your thesis statement? Write it here:

_____

_____

What is your short definition? Write it here:

_____

_____

Are you going to use any vocabulary expressions for definition? Note them here:

_____

_____

Paragraphs Two through ??:
The Development of Your Definition

The way you outline the body of your definition paper depends upon the way you plan to present your information. If, for example, you define this slang expression through examples, each paragraph might discuss a different example. If you define your expression through classification, each paragraph might discuss a different category of the slang expression's uses. You decide and then outline the body of your paper in the way you think is most appropriate. In each paragraph, include the following information:

What is the topic sentence for this paragraph? Write it here:

_____

_____

What important information should be in this paragraph? Write it here:

_____

_____

Are you going to use any vocabulary expressions for definition? Note them here:

_____

_____

Last Paragraph: The Conclusion

In the last paragraph, bring your definition to an end. Also try to make an interesting observation. You might, for example, want to note one time when you used the slang expression either correctly or incorrectly. You might want to state your opinion of this term. Do you think it is silly, funny, stupid, frivolous? Why? What interesting point would you like to add?

What is the topic sentence for this paragraph? Write it here:

_____

_____

What important information should be in this paragraph? Write it here:

_____

_____

Are you going to use any vocabulary expressions for definition? Note them here:

_____

_____

Rough Draft

Now using your notes, write the first draft of your composition.

Peer Editing

Find a partner and exchange your compositions. Follow these steps:

1. Read your partner's composition. Do not make any marks on the paper the first time you read it. Just try to get the main point.

2. Reread the paper. Underline any words, phrases, or expressions that don't seem correct or that are difficult to understand.

3. Do you have any questions about the contents of the composition? If so, write them on the Comments Sheet.

4. Now write three suggestions to the writer for improving his or her composition. Give the composition and Comments Sheet to your partner.

Writing Your Final Draft

First consider the points from your partner's Comments Sheet. Add them to your rough draft if needed. Then write the final draft of your composition.

Questions to Ask Yourself before Handing in Your Paper

Put a check mark in each box after you complete the tasks.

☐ Do I have a clear introduction with a good thesis statement?

☐ Do the body paragraphs clearly present in an organized manner the points I am trying to make?

☐ Does each paragraph have sufficient information so that the reader can understand what I am saying?

☐ Have I used appropriate definition vocabulary terms to help the information flow smoothly?

☐ Did I remember to include some well-structured complex and compound-complex sentences similar to the sample sentences in this chapter?

When you finish your composition, give it to your instructor. After your instructor evaluates your composition, discuss it with him or her. Both oral and written comments can be very helpful feedback when you are trying to assess the quality of your composition.

ADDITIONAL DEFINITION TOPICS

1. Define what, in your opinion, it means to be a serious student.

2. Define what, in your opinion, it means to be rich.

3. Define what it means to have trust.

4. Define what it means to be content or to be at peace with oneself.

5. Define what it means to be successful.

6. Define what it means to be a leader.

7. Define what it means, in your opinion, to be a good instructor of English.

10

Persuasion

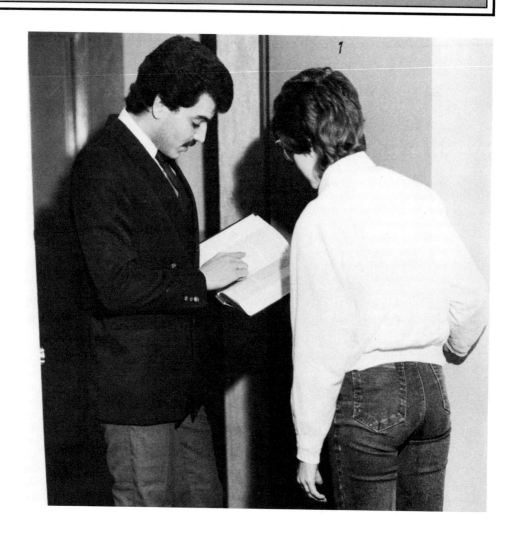

Sometimes when you write, you want to convince your readers to accept your point of view on a given subject. This is called *persuasion*. Consider, for example, the topic of legalizing the use of marijuana in the United States. In a persuasion paper, either you would take a stand *for* the legalization of marijuana or you would take a stand *against* it.

When you write a persuasion paper, you generally assume that your reader does not support your point of view. Your goal is to have your reader come to agree with your opinions by carefully building strong and convincing arguments for your side while tearing down or weakening the opposing side's.

To build your arguments and weaken the other's, use *facts, statistics,* and *examples* that are beyond your personal knowledge.

Facts: A fact is a piece of information that is objectively right. You can't argue about it.

EXAMPLE

The sun rises in the east and sets in the west.

Statistics: A statistic is a collection of numerical information regarding a particular topic.

EXAMPLE

Following are the four most popular fields of study at a local college that has approximately 11,000 students.

Top Four Fields in Order of Student Enrollment

1.	Computer Science	2,420
2.	Business	1,921
3.	Health Sciences	1,701
4.	Engineering	1,005

Examples: An example is a single item, fact, incident, or aspect that represents a general topic or subject. It can be stated briefly or in extended form.

EXAMPLE

The author Ayn Rand is internationally known for her philosophical writings. *Anthem, The Fountainhead,* and *Atlas Shrugged* are three of her most popular books.

Generally speaking, you present the arguments for your side and against the other side in two different ways: you appeal to the logic of your reader and/or you appeal to his or her emotions. When you appeal to the logic of your reader, you use evidence (facts, statistics, examples) beyond your own experience that is believable and has strong, unfaulty reasoning. The goal is to convince your reader that, logically speaking, your side of the issue is the only one that can be considered valid.

When trying to appeal to your reader's emotions, you support your opinions and weaken the other's by using dramatic experiences from your own life or from some other outside source. The goal is to persuade the reader that your side of the issue is correct by deeply touching one of his or her emotions. They can be negative emotions such as disgust, anger, or fear; they can be positive emotions such as compassion, excitement, or pity.

We need to consider two more points before attempting to write a persuasion paper. First, how does one state opposing arguments? Second, how can one properly give credit to other people's information in a persuasion paper when necessary?

STATING OPPOSING ARGUMENTS

When writing a persuasion paper, it is important not to forget to address the issues raised by those who hold the opposite view. It is not enough just to build a strong case for your side in the paper. By mentioning the opposite opinions, you can show the reader that you are aware of the other side's views and that you are not afraid to challenge the ones with which you disagree. It can also show that you are willing to look at both sides of an issue fairly and openly. You admit that you are willing to consider some points that do not agree with yours. This allows you to state that the opposing side makes some good points but that you feel the points on your side are as good or better.

Opposing arguments can appear throughout a persuasive paper. Often the opposing points of view are mentioned in the introduction. When a writer does this, the other side's opinions are mentioned in such a way as to make the writer's own thesis statement appear even stronger. Sometimes the writer decides to put the opposing arguments all in one paragraph, usually the paragraph immediately following the introduction. The rest of the paper then builds a case for the writer's side of the issue and weakens the other side's case mentioned in the second paragraph.

GIVING CREDIT TO OTHER PEOPLE'S INFORMATION

When you write a research paper, you will learn traditional ways to document resource information obtained from books, periodicals, interviews, and so on by using footnotes and making bibliographies. In the short persuasive essay, it is not necessary to use this traditional form of documentation for statistics, facts, or statements. It is important, however, to give credit to the person who gave the information and to mention from which source it came. Look at the following examples:

- In the November 1985 issue of *Living Well,* Bob Lewis stated, "A simple test for detecting cancer of the colon is now available for over-the-counter purchase at your local drug store. In a very short time, a person can find out if the test results are positive or negative. A positive result does not necessarily mean that the person has cancer, but it does mean that he needs to see a doctor right away." It is hoped that this simple and private test will help people catch colon problems before they become serious.

- Today the decision whether or not to attend a four-year college immediately is being questioned. Many prospective students are finding that the community college may not be such a bad deal after all. In the article "The Two-Year College Connection" (*Educational News,* January 1986) Vicki Smith explained why she decided to attend her local two-year college. "Once I examined my options, there really was no choice. The community college is going to cost half of what it would to attend the university. I can study the same courses in smaller-sized classes with more personal attention. What's more, I can live at home and continue to work. And at the end of my two years at the community college, a transfer counselor will help me make a smooth transition to the university."

EXERCISE 1: Persuasive Statements: Appealing to Logic or to Emotions?

Read the following statements. Decide if each one is appealing to your logic or your emotions. Discuss your answers as a group.

1. We have sent seven million dollars to help that country fight the horrible poverty there. Before we sent the money, 38 percent of the population lived below the poverty line. At present, 34 percent of the population still lives in poverty. We must consider some other means of help. Financial assistance is just not working effectively.

LOGIC ✓   EMOTIONS

2. Just one time I wish you could see the badly cut, bruised, and bleeding face of a child who was hurt in a car accident because he was not wearing a seat belt. I know then that you would support my conviction that wearing seat belts should be made mandatory in this state.

LOGIC   EMOTIONS ✓

3. Last night when I came back from the grocery store, the thunderstorm was really strong. I walked into the house to find the electricity cut off and my ten-year-old son huddled in a corner of the kitchen crying and rocking back and forth. I will never forget that look of terror in his eyes as he screamed, "Mommy, I couldn't see anything! I was so afraid." I decided then that a child should not be left unattended even for a short while.

LOGIC   EMOTIONS ✓

4. Inhaling the smoke of someone else's cigarette can be harmful. As an example, nitrogen dioxide, a very irritating gas found in cigarettes, can harm the lungs. Nitrogen dioxide levels of 5 ppm (parts per million) in the air are considered dangerous. Cigarette smoke contains 250 ppm. For this reason, I feel nonsmokers should have a right to protect themselves from being exposed to cigarette smoke in public.

LOGIC ✓   EMOTIONS

5. For the past six semesters, 55 percent of Ms. Brown's Calculus I class have failed, while in the three other Calculus I classes only between 3 and 5 percent have failed. It seems highly unlikely to me that so many students unable to understand Calculus I would find their way into Ms. Brown's class. For this reason, I disagree with her contention that she has no trouble teaching this course.

LOGIC ✓   EMOTIONS

6. In my department are six men and two women. Each person is required to do the same job. Last year each man received a 1,500-dollar raise while each woman received a 750-dollar raise. This suggests that some type of sexual discrimination is occurring here.

LOGIC ✓   EMOTIONS

7. When he walked up to the podium to speak, the crowd grew suddenly still. When he started to speak, every eye was glued to his face. As he gave his speech, the people followed his every word. They cheered and hollered at the right moments. They cried and moaned when the words demanded it. Never had I seen so many people absolutely captivated by one human being. His power, his strength, his ability to inspire could not be matched by anyone before the election. No counting of the votes was necessary. I knew that I was looking at the next president of the United States.

LOGIC   EMOTIONS ✓

EXERCISE 2: Distinguishing Between Faulty Logic and Sound Logic

---

When appealing to a reader's logic, you have to be sure that you use statements that have sound reasoning. It is easy, if you are not careful, to make a statement to prove a point that sounds logical but in reality has poor reasoning. Look at the statements that follow. Decide why each statement has either faulty or sound logic. Discuss your answers with the group.

S 1. Of the people who used this new arthritis drug, 45 percent experienced bad headaches every time they took a pill. There is a <u>strong possibility</u>, then, that the medicine is causing the headaches.

F 2. I can drive a car very well. So, I'm sure that I can drive an eighteen-wheel truck.

F 3. If Diana Ross, the singer, likes to wear Viking shoes, then they must be very comfortable.

S 4. Subscriptions to our daily newspaper are down by nearly <u>32 percent</u> this year. I think we can assume that our readers are becoming dissatisfied with it in some way.

F 5. Five girls who took a sex-education class last semester became pregnant. If they hadn't taken the course, they wouldn't have become pregnant.

F 6. When I applied for my credit card, they gave it to me right away. Anyone can get a credit card if he or she fills out the application correctly.

F 7. Sixteen-year-olds have never been allowed to vote in a state election. For this reason, they should not be permitted to do so now.

S 8. Every time she drank coffee, she broke out in little red spots on her face and arms. This never happened any other time. She must be allergic to something in coffee.

IMPORTANT VOCABULARY

The following words and phrases are commonly used in a persuasion paper. These expressions indicate that you are stating your personal opinions on an issue.

In my opinion,

From my point of view,

As I see it,

I think

I believe

I feel

I conclude

I am certain, sure, positive, convinced

I agree

I disagree

It seems, appears to me

My opinion is based on

EXAMPLES

I can *conclude* from the statistics just out that our business profits are going to decline this year.

Fastfood hamburgers are unhealthy to eat. *My opinion is based on* the fact that they are extremely high in fat, salt, and sugar.

As I see it, we have only one option. We must not permit the use of handguns by anyone but law-enforcement people.

EXERCISE 3: Practice Using Persuasion Vocabulary

In a group, take turns practicing the expressions provided in the preceding list. To begin, one student chooses an expression and a topic. That person calls on another person to use the expression by making a statement about the topic. For example:

Student 1: From my point of view (taxes)

Student 2: "From my point of view, taxes are not fairly distributed in this country."

Continue around the group until everyone has several chances to make statements.

IMPORTANT PUNCTUATION/USAGE:
Underlining Works, Quoting Works,
and Documenting Works

Here are some punctuation and style rules that are worth noting before writing a persuasion paper.

A. In English, we underline certain works, including the titles of books, periodicals (which include magazines), pamphlets, published speeches, movies, and television and radio programs.

EXAMPLES

The Kingdom by Robert Lacy   (book)

Time   (magazine)

The Empire Strikes Back   (movie)

B. We put quotation marks around certain material, including articles in periodicals, short stories, essays, and episodes of television and radio programs.

EXAMPLES

"Bony People" by Nancy Potter   (short story)

"The Season of Discontent" from Time   (news article)

C. To review how we quote a person in direct speech, reread the "Important Punctuation" section of chapter two.

D. Remember that in a persuasion paper when mentioning a periodical, an article in a periodical, a television or radio program, an episode of a television or radio program, or a published speech, it is also important to note the date and the year that the information was given. This makes it easier for your reader to follow up on the information if he or she desires.

EXAMPLES

In Senator Taylor's March 4, 1984, speech, he simply stated, "All funds for the new program will be cut off effective the last day of this month."

On November 8, 1983, the Youngstown Journal reported that the mayor had been arrested on charges of fraud.

---

*EXERCISE 4: Practice Using Correct Punctuation
When Citing Sources in a Persuasion Essay*

Practice using the punctuation and style rules by finding actual sources to cite. The examples should help you. When you finish, show your instructor.

EXAMPLE: (pamphlet, date) In July 1985 Thorton College published a pamphlet entitled "Foreign Students: Surviving in the U.S." It stated that 2 percent of the international students who come to study at their college return home during the first month of school.

1. (magazine article, date) _____

_____

2. (pamphlet, date) _____

_____

3. (television news program, date, person speaking) _____

_____

4. (newspaper article, date) _____

_____

5. (a person making a direct quotation) _____

_____

GUIDED WRITING ACTIVITY

Many cities in the United States are banning (not allowing) smoking in public places such as restaurants, sports arenas, and buses. Do you think this is a good idea or a bad one? Imagine that you had to try to persuade your local government either to allow smoking in public places or to ban it. Which side would you support?

Peer Interaction

A. Get into groups of three or four. Everyone in the group should either support public smoking or ban it.

B. STRATEGY FOR GATHERING INFORMATION

As a group, for about ten minutes, you are going to make a list (see page xiii for listmaking) of every reason you can think of why public smoking should be permitted or banned. Let your imagination go. Try to think of as many different reasons as you can.

C. Now think of your opponents' point of view. For about five minutes put yourself in your opponents' shoes and make a list of every reason you can think of why their side should be supported instead of yours. Try to think of as many different reasons as you can.

D. ANOTHER STRATEGY FOR GATHERING INFORMATION

Now take a few minutes to show your lists to a group in the class that is taking the opposite point of view. If, for example, your group supports public smoking, show your lists to a group that wants to ban it. Evaluate each other's lists. Did the other group forget any information that could be listed under your point of view? Did your group forget any information that could be put under the other side's point of view? Should some reasons be eliminated because they aren't strong enough? Discussing this information with the opposing side should help you see both sides clearly.

E. A THIRD STRATEGY FOR GATHERING INFORMATION

Remember that one part of writing a convincing persuasive paper is to mention and then dispute the other side of the argument. From step C you already have a list of reasons supporting the other side's views. Now to help you gather information to dispute your opponent's side, you are going to role play on paper (see page xiv for roleplaying). In other words, you are going to write a rough imaginary conversation between yourself and the opposing side. Follow these directions:

1. Take a piece of paper. Write down a reason why you do or do not support public smoking. Explain why you feel this way.

2. Reread the reason. Now for five minutes respond to the reasons as yourself, explaining why they are weak or invalid. Make comments and ask questions to the other side. Let your imagination go. Really "talk" to the "other person."

3. Continue steps 1 and 2 until you feel you have gathered enough information for your composition so that you can present and dispute the other person's side of this issue. The important thing to remember is that in step 1 you are writing as the opposing side. In step 2 you are writing as yourself.

4. When you finish the "conversation on paper," reread it carefully. Start to choose which information you want to use in your essay and which you don't.

F. Do you feel you are ready to begin working on a draft of your persuasion paper? If not, review steps A through E until you feel you can begin writing.

Organizing Your Information

1. Now think about the information you have gathered on permitting or banning public smoking.

2. Try to organize this information into a clear, concise essay. There are several ways to organize your reasons in a persuasive essay:

   a. You can make the reasons have equal value and list them in any order you want.

b. You can list the most important reason first, followed by the second most important reason, and finish with the least important reason.

c. You can list the least important reason first, followed by the second most important reason, and finish with the most important reason.

If you can't decide which way to use, discuss your reasons with your teacher. Then go ahead.

3. The outline that follows is a suggestion to get you started. If you would like to modify it to suit your needs better, discuss your idea with your teacher and then go ahead.

Paragraph One: Introduction to Public Smoking

Define public smoking. Mention whether you support or reject the idea of public smoking. Explain how you are going to persuade the local government to either ban or permit smoking in public places. Don't give a lot of detail. In the introduction, you just want to present the main idea to your reader.

What important information should be in your introduction? Write it here:

_____

_____

What is your thesis statement? Write it here:

_____

_____

Are you going to use any persuasion vocabulary terms? Note them here:

_____

_____

Paragraph Two: The Other Side's Point of View

What is the topic sentence of this paragraph? Write it here:

_____

_____

What points might the other side make to support its point of view? Write them here:

_____

_____

_____

Why are these reasons weak or less convincing than yours? Write your answer here:

_____

_____

Are you going to use any persuasion vocabulary terms? Note them here:

_____

_____

Paragraph Three: The First Reason to Support (Ban) Public Smoking

What is the topic sentence for this paragraph? Write it here:

_____

_____

What is the first reason to support (ban) public smoking? Explain it here:

_____

_____

What important details, examples, statistics, and facts are you going to use to make your reason convincing? List them here:

_____

_____

Are you going to use any persuasion vocabulary terms? Note them here:

_____

_____

Paragraph Four: The Third Reason to Support (Ban) Public Smoking

What is the topic sentence for this paragraph? Write it here:

_____

_____

What is the third reason to support (ban) public smoking? Explain it here:

_____

_____

What important details, examples, statistics, and facts are you going to use to make your reason convincing? List them here:

_____

_____

Are you going to use any persuasion vocabulary terms? Note them here:

_____

_____

Paragraph Five: (If Necessary) The Third Reason to Support (Ban) Public Smoking

What is the topic sentence for this paragraph? Write it here:

_____

_____

What is the third reason to support (ban) public smoking? Explain it here:

_____

_____

What important details, examples, statistics, and facts are you going to use to make your reason convincing? List them here:

_____

_____

Are you going to use any persuasion vocabulary terms? Note them here:

_____

_____

Paragraph Six: The Conclusion

In your conclusion, bring together the information from your introduction and body paragraphs. In addition, try to add an interesting point. You might want to discuss how accepting your point of view would directly benefit the people in the local government. You might want to make a prediction of what will happen in your city if the government does not adopt your point of view. What interesting point would you like to add?

What is your topic sentence? Write it here:

_____

_____

What important information should be in your conclusion? Write it here:

_____

_____

What interesting point would you like to add? Write it here:

_____

_____

Are you going to use any persuasion vocabulary terms? Note them here:

_____

_____

Rough Draft

Now using your notes, write the first draft of your composition.

Peer Editing

Find a partner and exchange your compositions. Follow these steps:

1. Read your partner's composition. Do not make any marks on the paper the first time you read it. Just try to get the main point.

2. Reread the paper. Underline any words, phrases, or expressions that don't seem correct or that are difficult to understand.

3. Do you have any questions about the contents of the composition? If so, write them on the Comments Sheet.

4. Now write three suggestions to the writer for improving his or her composition.

5. Give the composition and Comments Sheet to your partner.

Writing the Final Draft

First consider the points from your partner's Comments Sheet. Add them to your rough draft if needed. Then write the final draft of your composition.

Questions to Ask Yourself before Handing in Your Paper

Put a check mark in each box after you complete the tasks.

☐ Do I have a clear introduction with a good thesis statement?

☐ Do the body paragraphs clearly present in an organized manner the points I am trying to make?

☐ Does each paragraph have sufficient information so that the reader can understand what I am saying?

☐ Have I used persuasion vocabulary terms to help one idea flow smoothly into the next?

☐ If I cited any sources in my paper, did I remember to punctuate them correctly?

When you finish your composition, give it to your instructor. After your instructor evaluates your composition, discuss it with him or her.

ADDITIONAL PERSUASION TOPICS

1. Think of an important life choice a friend or family member is about to make (getting married, buying a house or car, changing jobs, and so on). Persuade that person that he or she is making the wrong decision.

2. Imagine that there is a job you really want. You were notified today that the field of applicants has been narrowed to two people and you are one of them. Write an essay that will be read at your final interview by the people hiring you. Convince them that they should select you for the position.

3. In the United States certain cities have begun to use nuclear power plants to help supply energy to the community. Imagine that the city in which you are now living is considering building a nuclear power plant. Present your arguments to the local board of public utilities to persuade them either to build or not to build the plant where you live. You will probably need to do some reading on this subject before you write your paper.

4. Write a paper in which you persuade the reader that a person should (should not) be allowed to have a handgun in his or her home.

5. Imagine that you work in a large grocery store in a neighborhood that has many elderly people living in it. Today you caught an old man stealing some food because, he says, he didn't have enough money to pay for it. You can let the man go or call the police and press charges. Which would you do? Write a paper in which you convince the reader which action is best.

6. Imagine that your family wants you to study _____ at the university. **(a subject)**

   You, however, would rather study _____. Persuade your family that **(a subject)**

   you should study the subject you want instead of the one they want.

7. Pick a law that is handled differently in your country than in North America (for example, the legal age for driving, the legal age for drinking, the punishment for stealing, the legal age for voting). Explain how the law is handled in each country and persuade your reader which you think is better and why.

Problem Solving

Sometimes when you write a paper you want to identify, define, and then solve a problem. This is called *problem solving*. We have to solve problems all the time. We may have to figure out how to settle an argument over a bill with a credit company, for example. Or we may have to try to live on one thousand dollars this month when we actually need fifteen hundred. We may even have to decide how to continue our education although our parents can no longer afford to pay for it.

Sometimes we can solve problems by thinking alone or by discussing them with others. Other times we need to solve the problem on paper. Learning how to present a problem in written form and how to offer a reasonable solution for it can be a valuable communication tool for you to have.

SOLVING A PROBLEM ON PAPER

When a person wants to solve a problem in written form, there is a system or series of steps he or she generally follows. Here are the steps:

First: *State the problem.* Briefly, clearly, and simply explain exactly what the problem is.

Second: *Define the problem.* Explain in some detail the information regarding this problem. Keep in mind that you are trying to limit, or set boundaries for, your definition. What makes this problem different from all other problems?

Third: *Suggest possible solutions.* The next step is to present several, generally at least three, possible solutions to your problem. These can be the strongest solutions you can think of, the most commonly accepted solutions to the problem, or solutions that have been suggested to you by someone else. In this step you just present the solutions; you do not state which is the best.

Fourth: *Judge the solutions.* In this step you discuss the strong and weak points of the solutions. You want your reader to understand as clearly as you do why one solution is better than the others.*

Fifth: *Recommend the best solution.* The last step, often written in the conclusion, is to state directly which of the solutions you think is best and why. This can be done very briefly because if you have done step 4 correctly, your reader should know which solution you have chosen. Specifically, recommending the best solution to the problem helps bring the paper to a definite finish.

---

*Sometimes it is not possible to find a solution to a problem. In these cases you explain why you believe no solution to the problem is possible. Point out the weaknesses of the best solution to support your point.

Where to Find Information

How do you gather information when looking for a solution to your problem? Generally there are two ways: through what we see or know and through what others tell us.

When we say that we get information through what we see or know, we mean that we get it through past experience and knowledge, by observing, and by experimentation. When we say that we get the information from what others tell us, we mean that we get it by such means as interviews, questionnaires, discussions, and research.

Some Hints for Successful Problem Solving

When gathering information, it is important to listen to people carefully, to take good notes, and to be as objective as possible. To be objective means to present the facts of the problem and its solution the way they truly are and not the way you want them to be to help your paper. Also, try to keep an open mind when gathering information. Remember that problem solving is a process to help you find the best solution to a problem. If you think you have the best answer before you get started, you may miss some valuable information.

EXERCISE 1: Practice Identifying the Steps
in Problem Solving

In this activity you are going to identify the different steps in written problem solving. Read each of the groups of information that follow. Identify each group as being one of the following:

- Statement of the Problem
- Definition of the Problem
- Possible Solutions to the Problem
- Evaluation of the Problem
- Recommendation of the Best Solution to the Problem

1. One solution might be to ask my coworker not to smoke. Another solution might be to move my desk so that I don't sit as near to my smoking coworker. Another solution might be to ask to move to another office where people don't smoke. A final, but not very practical, way to resolve this problem would be to start smoking myself.

Step: _____

2. A major problem at the office is that workers who don't smoke must share offices with people who do.

Step: _____

3. Let me give you some background on this problem. My coworker and I share an office that is about ten feet by twelve feet in size. Because of the nature of our jobs, we must work together from time to time. My coworker says that she needs to smoke because it makes her feel less nervous. I can't stand to breathe cigarette smoke because I have asthma. Cigarette smoke makes it difficult for me to breathe. As of yet, our company has no policy that prohibits smoking in the offices.

Step: _____

4. After looking at all the possible solutions, I feel that the best one is to ask if I can move to another office to work. If my coworker is forced to quit smoking, her ability to work will be hurt. If I have to continue to smell smoke, my ability to work will be lessened. We can agree to meet at a "neutral location" for short periods of time when we need to work together. My coworker will not smoke during those times. In this way we can both do our jobs and be happy in our working environments.

Step: _____

5. Of course, it is not possible to assume that my coworker will quit her job just because I don't like the fact that she smokes. I am not prepared to quit my job either. I am certainly not going to take up smoking, since I am an asthmatic. So, let's look now at the more workable solutions. I could ask my coworker not to smoke. This doesn't seem to be the best solution. It would probably make her angry. Even if she agreed to try, there is no guarantee that she would be successful. We work in a high-pressure job, and she says that she smokes to help relieve tension. I considered moving my desk to a different corner in the room so that I was no longer facing my coworker's desk. This doesn't seem like a very good solution because I will still be able to inhale the smoke no matter where I am in the room. This would also probably make my coworker angry because I would constantly be reminding her that I don't like her smoking.

Step: _____

6. The best solution to this problem appears to be to contact the gas company and let them know that you cannot afford the large rate increase in gas for heat. Then you and the gas company can begin to make plans for you to pay the bills at a rate you can afford.

Step: _____

7. Simply stated, the problem is that my neighbor does not have enough money to pay the increased rates in the gas bill this month.

Step: _____

8. A possible solution would be not to pay the bill and see what happens. Another solution would be to take out a loan to help pay for the increase in the gas rates. My neighbor could also quit using heat and rely on his fireplace and electric heaters to keep warm. He could also let the gas company know immediately that he can pay some, but not all, of the bill. He could then ask the company to help him set up a payment plan that is workable for him and the company.

Step: _____

9. My neighbor lives in an older, energy-inefficient home. He is retired and has a limited income. This year the gas company increased its rates for heating by 9 percent. It has been a very cold winter this year. Yesterday Mr. Larson told me that he can't afford to pay his last gas bill. He is very worried that the gas company is just going to shut off his gas with no warning. He doesn't know what to do.

Step: _____

10. I don't recommend that my neighbor just ignore the bill and wait to see what happens. The gas company is a business. If the customer doesn't pay, the business will stop providing the gas. There will be no communication between the company and the customer. Because my neighbor just quit paying his bill without an explanation, he will from that point on be considered a credit risk. It will be difficult for him to get credit from companies to pay other bills.

It is also not a very wise idea to take out a loan to pay for the heating bills. My neighbor has a limited income because he is retired. He probably couldn't get a loan even if he tried. If by chance he got the loan, my neighbor would have to pay back the loan with interest. This means that he would be responsible for paying out even more money than now, which he doesn't have.

Using the fireplace and electric heaters is a better idea than the first two. For some people, it might even be the best solution. For my neighbor, however, it just isn't practical. He is an older man and isn't able to cut, stack, and carry large amounts of wood to keep the fireplace working. Also, his house is not well built. For this reason the fireplace and heaters might keep some areas warm, but the house would still be chilly and drafty, which is not healthy for an older person.

This leaves, then, the solution where my neighbor contacts the gas company, explains the situation, and tries to work out a payment plan that is agreeable to him and to the company.

Step: _____

EXERCISE 2: Distinguishing between Objective and Subjective Statements

---

In this exercise you are given some information about a problem. Following it are several statements. Decide which statements are presented objectively and which are presented subjectively. Remember that to present information objectively means to present it the way it really is. To present the information subjectively means to present it in a way that is distorted by personal feelings or prejudices. Read each statement carefully. If the statement is objective, mark an *O* by it. If the statement is subjective, mark an *S* by it.

PROBLEM: It is time for Christopher to go to college. He wants to be an engineer. He received all A's and B's in high school and now wants to get the best education possible. There are two schools in his state that he can attend. One school (University A) has an excellent engineering department that is known nationally, but the tuition is very expensive. The other school has an average engineering department. It is not excellent, but it is well known in the state. The tuition is less than half of the first school's. Christopher doesn't know which school to attend.

_____ 1. It costs $4,000 a semester to attend university A. It costs $1,200 a semester to attend university B.

_____ 2. The engineering department at university A is known throughout the country.

_____ 3. Anyone with brains would choose the best engineering department regardless of how much the tuition.

_____ 4. Christopher's grades in high school were all right, but I've seen better.

_____ 5. It is widely assumed that the lower the tuition at a university, the lower the quality of instruction a student will receive.

_____ 6. Christopher doesn't know whether it's wiser to attend a nationally known but expensive engineering program or a statewide-known but inexpensive program.

_____ 7. The reason Christopher can't make up his mind is that he is too cheap to pay the tuition for university A.

_____ 8. Christopher is eighteen years old. He just finished high school. He is getting ready to attend college.

_____ 9. Christopher shouldn't dream of attending a school that he can't afford.

_____ 10. Christopher plans to be an engineer.

IMPORTANT VOCABULARY

The following words and phrases are commonly used in a problem-solving paper:

I (strongly) suggest
One should, ought to
I (strongly) recommend
I advise you to
It would be a good idea to, for
I propose

EXAMPLES

I strongly recommend that you and your professor try to work out your problems before going to the dean.

It would be a good idea for you and your professor to work out your problems before going to the dean.

It would be a good idea to work out your problems before going to the dean.

Also commonly used in a problem-solving paper are these phrases:

One { idea / solution / suggestion / plan / proposal / strategy / piece of advice / recommendation } is

EXAMPLES

One solution is to hire a person to paint the house and do the lawnwork. This would give you more free time.

One piece of advice is to hire a person to paint the house and do the lawnwork. This would give you more free time.

EXERCISE 3: Practice Using Problem-Solving Vocabulary

Practice writing sentences using the problem-solving vocabulary presented in this chapter. Write your sentences using the topics in parentheses.

EXAMPLE

(a problem with credit cards) *I advise you to cut up all of your credit cards and never use them again.*

1. (a problem with a job) _____

_____

2. (a friend is sick) _____

_____

3. (flunked a test) _____

_____

4. (a problem with the police) _____

_____

5. (receiving obnoxious phone calls every night) _____

_____

6. (bought something defective from a furniture store) _____

_____

7. (a problem with a spouse or boyfriend or girlfriend) _____

_____

8. (someone is homesick) _____

_____

9. (a friend has started telling lies) _____

_____

IMPORTANT PUNCTUATION/USAGE:
General Review of the Comma

Learning how to master the use of the comma in English can be difficult. Sometimes we want to put the comma into a sentence where it isn't needed. Other times we forget to put it into a sentence when it should be there. We even try to use the comma when we should be using some other kind of punctuation such as periods, colons, or semicolons. Here are presented some basic rules to follow when using the comma. Discuss them with your teacher.

A. Use a comma between a series of words or phrases.

EXAMPLES

She washed, dried, and put away the dishes.

The camp director brought soap, shampoo, suntan lotion, and sunglasses.

The nurse listened to the little boy's complaints quietly, patiently, and calmly.

B. Use a comma to separate words or phrases that are added to a sentence. This additional material can be at the beginning, in the middle, or at the end of the sentence.

EXAMPLES

Luckily, we had just enough money to pay the bus driver.

The only way to learn to speak a second language, as far as I'm concerned, is to live in a country where it is spoken.

That little boy isn't stupid, just shy around strangers.

C. Use a comma to separate nonessential (nonrestrictive) information in a sentence.

EXAMPLES

My house, which is tan and blue, needs to be repainted.

My mother, who is the president of the club, delivered the first speech.

NOTE: If the information is essential or restricts the sentence, then no commas should separate it from the rest of the sentence. Look at the following two sentences. The sentence with commas has a different meaning from the sentence without commas.

My house, which is tan and blue, needs to be repainted.

My house which is tan and blue needs to be repainted.

In the first sentence, the important information is that this person's house needs to be repainted. It is only incidental that the house is blue and tan. The second sentence implies that the person has more than one house. The house that needs to be repainted is the blue and tan one, not the gray and white one, for example. Knowing the color of the house is essential to the meaning of the sentence. For this reason, the information is not separated from the sentence by commas. Can you explain the difference between the next two sentences?

My car, which is a two-door convertible, just got a flat tire.

My car which is a two-door convertible just got a flat tire.

D. Place a comma before a coordinating expression (and, but, or, nor, yet, for, so) that is joining two complete thoughts. (Review chapter four, pages 61 and 62.)

EXAMPLES

John moved the piano into the middle of the stage, and Ellen moved the chair next to it.

Don rented an apartment, but his brother Bob bought a house.

NOTE: Do not use a comma before a coordinating expression if the second thought is not a complete one.

EXAMPLES

I finished the composition and started my next assignment.

Alice bought the ticket for the concert but didn't attend.

NOTE: Do not use a comma to separate two complete thoughts unless they are joined by a coordinating expression. Use a period or a semicolon.

EXAMPLES

LeRoy will bring the salad to the party. Carolyn will bring the meat.

Alison likes to study in the park; Adam likes to study in his room.

E. Use a comma to separate a subordinate clause from a main clause if the subordinate clause comes *before* the main clause. (Review chapter nine, on page 139.)

EXAMPLE

Unless I find a part-time job, I won't be able to pay my rent next month.
Before I got on the plane, I waved one last time to my parents.

NOTE: If a subordinate clause comes *after* the main clause, do not use a comma.

EXAMPLES

I won't be able to pay my rent next month unless I find a part-time job.
I waved one last time to my parents before I got on the plane.

EXERCISE 4: Practice Making Sentences Needing Commas

In this exercise you are going to practice creating your own sentences that need commas. Review the preceding information to help you. Share your sentences with the others in your class when you finish.

Write three sentences using commas in a series.

1. _____

_____

2. _____

_____

3. _____

_____

Write three sentences to which you add material. This material can be added to the beginning, in the middle, or at the end of the sentence.

1. _____

_____

2. _____

_____

3. _____

_____

Write three sentences to which you add nonessential (nonrestrictive) information.

1. _____

_____

2. _____

_____

3. _____

_____

Write three sentences. Each sentence must have two complete ideas that are joined by a coordinating expression.

1. _____

_____

2. _____

_____

3. _____

_____

Write three sentences. Each sentence must have two ideas joined by a coordinating expression. One idea is *complete;* the other idea is *not complete.*

1. _____

_____

2. _____

_____

3. _____

_____

Write three sentences. Each sentence has a subordinating clause and a main clause.

1. _____

_____

2. _____

_____

3. _____

_____

GUIDED WRITING ACTIVITY

In this writing activity you are going to imagine that you are a student who usually makes good grades. In a course you are presently taking, however, you are not getting the grades you expected. It is very important to you to find a way to start getting better grades in the course.

Because you are just getting acquainted with problem solving on paper in English, in this chapter your problem-solving writing activity is neither too complex nor too technical. Use your own experience and knowledge and group discussions to gather most of your information. You do not need to do a lot of research or experimentation.

Peer Interaction

A. Get into groups of three or four. As a group decide on the course in which you are doing poorly. If, for example, it is an English course, decide which specific subject you are having trouble with: reading, vocabulary, composition, discussion, and so on.

B. STRATEGY FOR GATHERING INFORMATION

For the next ten or fifteen minutes brainstorm about possible ways to make higher grades in this course (see page xii for brainstorming). At this point, remember, you are not trying to decide which solution is better than the others. You just want to come up with as many solutions as possible.

C. ANOTHER STRATEGY FOR GATHERING INFORMATION

As a group or individually, identify two people who have experience and knowledge helping people who are doing poorly in classes. You are going to interview them (see page xiii for interviewing). For example, you might want to consider talking to your teacher, an advisor, a school tutor, or some other person. Ask each person the following questions. Listen carefully to the answers and take good notes.

1. What ways do you suggest that I could use to improve my failing grades in
_____?

       (course name)

2. Which of these suggestions do you think is the best? Why?

3. Why aren't the other suggestions as helpful?

4. (Add any other question you would like to ask.)

D. As a group combine your brainstorming suggestions with those of the experienced people with whom you talked. You should have a fairly good list of suggestions by now.

E. Try to evaluate each solution. Make note of each suggestion's strong points and weak points. By the end of your discussion, you should have a good idea of which suggestion for improving your grade is the best and why. You should also have a good idea of why the others are not as effective or helpful.

F. Do you feel you have enough information to begin working on a draft of your essay? Can you present and evaluate clearly and completely each suggestion you are going to use in your paper? If not, review steps A through E until you feel you can begin writing.

Organizing Your Information

1. In this writing activity you are going to organize your own information instead of following a sample outline as you have done in the other chapters.

2. Look at all your notes. Make an outline of how you would like to organize the information. Make sure you include each of the following steps:

Stating the problem

Defining the problem

Suggesting possible solutions

Evaluating the solutions

Recommending the best solutions

3. Share your outline with your instructor or another person in the class. Use these questions to help you check each other's outlines.

a. Are the divisions of the material logical?

b. Does the outline have an introduction, body, and conclusion?

c. Does the outline have a thesis statement in the introduction?

d. Does each major division of the outline seem to have enough information?

e. Can you offer any suggestions to help the writer improve his or her outline?

Rough Draft

Now using your notes, write the first draft of your composition.

Peer Editing

Find a partner and exchange your compositions. Follow these steps:

1. Read your partner's composition. Do not make any marks on the paper the first time you read it. Just try to get the main point.

2. Reread the paper. Underline any words, phrases, or expressions that don't seem correct or that are difficult to understand.

3. Do you have any questions about the contents of the composition? If so, write them on the Comments Sheet.

4. Now write three suggestions to the writer for improving his or her composition.

5. Give the composition and Comments Sheet to your partner.

Writing Your Final Draft

First consider the points from your partner's Comments Sheet. Put them into your rough draft if needed. Then write the final draft of your composition.

Questions to Ask Yourself before Handing in Your Paper

Put a check mark in each box after you complete the tasks.

☐ Do I have a clear introduction with a good thesis statement?

☐ Do the paragraphs clearly present the points I am trying to make?

☐ Does each paragraph have enough information so that the reader can understand what I am saying?

☐ Have I used problem-solving vocabulary to help one idea flow smoothly into the next?

☐ Did I remember to use the comma correctly in any sentence that requires one?

When you finish your composition, give it to your instructor. After your instructor evaluates your composition, discuss it with him or her.

ADDITIONAL PROBLEM-SOLVING TOPICS

1. You never had a weight problem. In the past few months, however, you have put on a lot of weight that you can't seem to lose. Write a paper in which you offer the best solution to losing unwanted pounds.

2. Over the past year the number of crimes has risen dramatically in your neighborhood. Write a paper in which you offer the best solution to decrease the number of crimes where you live.

3. Imagine that you have a friend who has a very low opinion of himself or herself due to an unhappy childhood. Write a paper in which you offer the best solution to help your friend get a strong self-image.

4. Imagine that there is a required course at your school that you must take. You do not like the teacher at all. What do you do?

5. Imagine that you have an abnormal fear of heights (dark places, spiders, flying, or whatever). Write a paper in which you offer the best solution to get rid of this problem.

6. Imagine that you received a bill from a furniture company that says you owe them 500 dollars for some furniture that you bought last month. Your name is on the bill, but you have never even been inside that store. You have never bought any furniture there. Write a paper in which you offer the best solution to this problem.

7. Imagine that you have a roommate. You have lived together for about six months and things are not running very smoothly between you. The major problem, as you see it, is that you and your roommate are opposites. You are a day person while he or she is a night person. You get up and go to bed early. He or she gets up and goes to bed very late. You like to eat three regular meals a day. Your roommate likes to snack all day. You like classical music; your roommate likes rock and roll. And so on. Because of the conflicts, you are very unhappy with your present living situation. You also realize, however, that it would be both expensive and difficult to move, so this is not a decision you can make lightly. How would you solve the problem of lifestyle conflicts between you and your roommate?

12

A Final Look: Extra Practice in Writing the Short Essay

Choose one of the thesis statements, essay topics, or general subjects presented in this chapter. Develop your choice into an interesting short essay. These ideas are unguided. Use what you have learned about the writing process to help you put the ideas into essay form. In review, keep in mind each of the following:

1. Choose one or more of the writing strategies you've learned to help you gather information and ideas (brainstorming, listmaking, interviewing, and so on).

2. Organize the basic ideas into an outline.

3. Decide which writing pattern or patterns best help you express your ideas (cause and effect, illustration, persuasion, and so on).

4. Get help and comments from peers and knowledgeable people as often as possible during the writing process.

5. Be sure that you have a strong thesis statement or central idea.

6. Pay attention to unity, coherence, paragraph structure, sentence structure, and spelling.

7. Plan to write and rewrite your composition until you feel that it expresses what you want.

THESIS STATEMENTS

1. If a person follows these crucial steps, he or she can start his or her own small business.

2. I never dreamed repeating that rumor would cause so much trouble.

3. Not everyone has to go to college in order to have a successful career.

4. There are several different types of nurses in North American hospitals. The amount of education and the type of training they have received determine what their responsibilities are.

5. When describing one's favorite holiday, it is important to focus on how it originated, how it is celebrated, and why it is so special.

6. My country can claim several effective leaders. For the following reasons, however, _____ is generally considered to have been

   (leader's name)

   the most effective in bringing about important social changes for the general public.

7. The way I see myself is quite different from the way most people see me.

8. The last humorous (dramatic, action, and so on) film I saw was very memorable because of its excellent story, realistic acting, and interesting scenery.

9. If you ever find yourself unexpectedly out of a job, there are certain steps you should take to get back on your feet again.

10. Today we are bombarded with so much news from so many sources that we don't know how to absorb it all.

11. Economic aid for a society's unfortunate citizens (the poor, the physically handicapped, the mentally ill, and so on) should come from the government. (If you wish, take the opposite view that the aid should come from private and business sources.)

12. The punishment for stealing is different in my country than it is in North America. (If you wish, choose another crime for which a person is punished differently in your country than in North America.)

13. Parents should limit the amount of television their children watch. (If you wish, take the opposite view.)

14. Often, when there is a discussion on current music, its negative qualities are mentioned. However, it is also important to note that popular music sends positive messages to the people who listen to it.

15. Participatory sports can be divided into those that we play alone, in pairs, and in teams. What we learn about competition in sports depends on which of these types we are playing.

ESSAY TOPICS

1. Being assertive is different from being aggressive

2. Why are there so many poor people in a country this rich? (Or discuss any other irony you have noticed in North American society)

3. A hobby that is useful

4. A game (sport) played in my country that is not played in North America

5. A current fad in North America that I like (or, a current fad in North America that I think is silly)

6. The most effective way to relax

7. Rules at my school that I must follow but hate

8. Public transportation in ————————— is excellent (or terrible)
   (city name)

9. Serious problems with the credit system in North America

10. A time when I trusted someone but shouldn't have

11. Traveling safely during a winter storm

12. The treatment of international students at ————————— by
   (school name)

    North American students, instructors, and staff

13. An objective account of a serious car accident (This account can be of a fictional or real car accident)

14. You haven't lived until you've tried —————————! (Write an
    (The brand name of your favorite drink or food)

    advertisement for this product)

15. Ways to put yourself through college (if your family can't)

GENERAL SUBJECTS

These subjects are too broad to be successfully covered in a two-page to three-page essay. Limit the subject by writing an essay on just one part of it. Starting with a very general subject can be fun because you, the writer, decide what part is going to be discussed and how it is going to be presented.

1. A person who had a strong impact on history such as Einstein, Napoleon, Edison, Buddha, Ghandi, or Martin Luther King, Jr.

2. UFOs (Unidentified Flying Objects)

3. Prejudice

4. Mysteries of the pyramids

5. Solar heating (or passive heating)

6. Civil engineering

7. Caring for the aged

8. Polygamy versus monogamy

9. The NASA shuttle flights

10. Golf (tennis, soccer, football, baseball, basketball, and so on)

11. Advertising on television

12. Bad habits

13. White-collar crime (Ask your teacher to explain this expression if you are not familiar with it.)

14. The U.S. stock exchange

15. Communicating nonverbally

Index